CONVERSATIONS

Also by Hannah Ward and Jennifer Wild:

Celebrating Women (with Janet Morley) (SPCK, 1995)
Human Rites (Cassell, 1995)
Guard the Chaos (DLT, 1995)
The Lion Christian Quotation Collection (Lion, 1997)

CONVERSATIONS

Meeting our forebears in faith

HANNAH WARD
and JENNIFER WILD

First published in Great Britain 1997
Society for Promoting Christian Knowledge
Holy Trinity Church
Marylebone Road
London NW1 4DU

British Library Cataloguing-in-Publication Data
A catalogue record for this book is available from the British Library

ISBN 0-281-05056-2

Typeset by Wilmaset Ltd, Birkenhead, Wirral
Printed in Great Britain by
The Cromwell Press, Melksham, Wiltshire

CONTENTS

INTRODUCTION

How do we relate to those who have gone before us as people of faith – to their ideas, their dreams, their prayers? Are they simply 'the past' – part of what has happened but not necessarily of any relevance today? Or are they saints, role models, visionaries whom we long to learn from and imitate? Probably they are both and neither: they, just like us, are complex creatures.

This book of prayer and reflection attempts a conversation – or, rather, a whole series of conversations. This is not an altogether strange idea for Christians, who are used to the notion of prayer as conversation with God. Even if some teachers of prayer are keen to keep us from being overly attached to words and images, probably most of us at least *sometimes* 'talk' to God as we would to a friend. However, in the following pages we have embarked on another conversation, the kind you can have with a group of friends or acquaintances – though perhaps not so commonly in the age of television, electronic mail and the telephone. On the whole we are more used to watching and hearing the conversations of others – on Albert Square, in Ramsey Street or at the station in Sun Hill – than we are to 'making' our own conversation.

Even more difficult, it seems, is real communication with those of previous ages, even where they have shared the same Christian faith. We are still often caught somewhere between an excessively reverential approach to the saints and almost complete neglect of 'dead Christians'. But there is a kind of conversation we can have with any who have lived, where 'God is the third' (in Aelred's words) who gets conversation going. In such exchanges we begin to listen to the voices of those who have preceded us; we start to engage with God in each other, often because of our forebears' *unlikeness* to us; and our ongoing communication with God may change as a result of what we hear.

An example: one of the two compilers of this book spent a good many years as a member of a religious community which set out to follow the way of Clare of Assisi in an Anglican setting. As a result, she has a strongish sense of a long-term conversation with someone who has been dead for well over 700 years. This sense of companionship obviously arose from pursuing with others a way of life similar to Clare's, however different the setting; and the very settledness of place, the earthedness of it, whether in Assisi or in

Oxfordshire, was the clear focus for this friendship – communal, developing, spacious and ongoing.

Those of previous times and different cultures can be all the more interesting because of their unpredictability – especially if we are not trying to agree with them, but listening to them, speaking with them, finding those places and moments when new awareness surfaces, or old truths take on fresh colour, or even when we can say with relief, 'Thank God we don't need to think like that any more in order to be human and Christian!' There is something in these encounters which forms an important ingredient in our laying hold of life in the risen Jesus, the one who 'revealed the resurrection by rising to new life'. If in one sense the great 'cloud of witnesses' is massively silent, in another quite proper sense their voices can always be heard – and we can at times join in the conversation.

This can be true also of our own dead. As Brother Lothian SSF once suggested (p. 88), we can be more or less secretly relieved when another's life is finished, and we think that at least we no longer have to struggle with *that* difficult relationship. It can be an alarming thought that work still remains for us to do, that we are still connected with these people who, in their own way, are going to 'reveal the resurrection' to us who believe not just in the 'Christ of faith' (to use the theological catchphrase), but in the Jesus of faith, the one who has gone before us, like all who have finished their earthly life. And the same can be said when our feelings are prevailingly those of sorrow and loss.

So in this book you never know who you are going to bump into. To make the encounters as random as possible we have kept the order of names alphabetical: man and woman, housemaid and scholar, monk and bishop's wife, seeker and social critic. Within an admittedly limited 'western' range, there is some sense of a world outside our own shores, whatever these shores are. You may sometimes find similar images used on consecutive pages – an opportunity to imagine what the two people concerned might have had to say to each other ...

The ingredients of these conversations are: a brief description of the person quoted; a short passage from their writings; some verses from the Scriptures, either the Hebrew or Christian Testament, which bear some relation to the quotation above; a prayer written by one of us, based on reflection on these two passages; and finally a one-line comment.

Of these, the prayer is the part which could be put on one side, if you can find your own conversation with God without its help. Or it may offer yet another voice in the human conversation, still leaving you free to make your own prayer, at the time of reading or later in the day when reflection on the subject-matter leads towards this. The prayers are not pieces of polished liturgical writing, but simply the results of our own involvement in the conversation.

In any case, we hope to spark off ideas, and disagreement as well as prayer, and laughter, or at least a chuckle – the ingredients, after all, of a good conversation.

Prayer and laughter can belong together – and not only in the context of the currently well-publicized 'Toronto blessing'. Alan Watts (see p. 96), influenced no doubt by his Buddhist reading and encounters, gives one recipe for the lightheartedness which has a place in the life and prayer of the Christian. In some of its varied tones, the one-liner at the end of each page also refuses to leave the day's theme top-heavy with seriousness or weighed down by its own sobriety. In all cases we would be glad to think that you might join in by adding your own words to the conversation.

To talk together, we have to listen. Nowadays we tend to be rather fussy about whom we relate to from the past. Augustine, Tertullian and Co. are out of favour on the whole, while Hildegard, Mechtild and Eckhart enjoy a major come-back. Unless a voice from the past seems to speak directly to our present concerns, we are unlikely to take much notice of it. But if we talk only with those who think as we do, conversations can easily become trite and self-congratulatory. We all need to widen our capacity to meet people with different points of view. One rather neglected way of practising this is by setting ourselves to listen, and to listen hard, to what those who have gone before us have said. And often our attention is rewarded: we are unexpectedly illuminated; an old idea is given a new twist; and we find both new friends and more of ourselves in the past.

This is not to underestimate the problems of relating to others over time. This kind of listening is not easy, and all kinds of things get in the way – theology, language, different cultures, attitudes and audiences. Listening to anyone is hard enough; listening to someone across three or four centuries (even thirty or forty years) requires the sort of generous listening in which we must put aside our prejudices and immediate personal agendas. To allow this sense of hearing to be sharpened, we have confined the opening extracts to the writings of people who are no longer alive. They may have lived many centuries ago, or have died within the last few years – but they are all separated from us by this very clear gulf, and at the same time they are still there for us in memory, in their writings, and in their Christian or human companionship on the life-journey in which we are all engaged.

We have chosen passages which seem to us worth this effort of listening. The authors are not always the obvious great ones among Christian writers, nor have we necessarily used their most often-quoted remarks. Our preference was for views which are of common interest, arising out of the general experience of everyday, rather than specially gifted or privileged experiences. Clearly our sources had to be literate, or there would be nothing to quote directly from them. And the further back in time, the fewer are the women's writings from which to choose. Even a religious library stopping thirty or forty years ago looks extraordinarily male-dominated, and we have not yet reached the stage when it is easy to find fifty pieces by each sex, even of contemporary writing. But we hope that an interesting selection results from setting those limits to our choice, and believe that the present collection can offer pleasurable scope for this work of listening – which is in the end the basis both for prayer and understanding.

Hannah Ward
Jennifer Wild

AELRED OF RIEVAULX · *Friendship*

Aelred of Rievaulx (c.1110–67), the son of a Saxon priest in Hexham, spent some years in the Scottish royal court before joining the Cistercian house at Rievaulx, where he later became abbot.

This is real friendship at its highest, utterly faithful and indestructible; it is not corrupted by envy, or diminished by suspicion, or dissolved by ambition; if tempted in these ways it does not give in, under attack it stands firm, and can be seen to do so, even when subject over and over again to harsh criticism and battered by the many wrongs done to it. So, then, 'Go and do likewise'. But remember, friends are equals, and serve each other freely.

(*On Spiritual Friendship*)

I do not call you servants any longer, because the servant does not know what the master is doing; but I have called you friends, because I have made known to you everything that I have heard from my Father. (John 15.15)

> May we recognize friendship as a gift,
> and love to let our friends go free,
> prizing both nearness and distance,
> community of tastes and startling diversity,
> in the hope that
> what begins with individuals
> may end with societies and nations.

THE ONLY WAY TO HAVE A FRIEND IS TO BE ONE.
(Ralph Waldo Emerson)

FLORENCE ALLSHORN · *Looser and lighter*

Florence Allshorn (1887–1950), missionary in Uganda, and later a trainer of missionaries, was the founder of St Julian's, the outcome of 'a dream of a house in some lovely quiet place where [missionaries] could come and be quiet and rest and read and talk – where things could be refreshed and recreated ... and [a place] open for home people as well who needed to stop and know God again'.

I don't think you will get out by being gooder, but by flinging something to the winds. Don't pray to be made gooder, but to be made looser and lighter. It's the poets and lovers who get there.

(From a letter)

Ho, everyone who thirsts,
come to the waters,
and you that have no money,
come, buy and eat!
Come, buy wine and milk
without money and without price ...
Incline your ear, and come to me;
listen, so that you may live. (Isaiah 55.1, 3)

> Shake out our anxious, careful minds
> as you shake out the heavens,
> and expose the bright stars
> that you have made to shine in us.

GIVE ME ONE WHO LOVES: THEY KNOW WHAT I MEAN.
(Augustine of Hippo)

W. H. AUDEN · *Reticence*

Wystan Hugh Auden (1907-73), English-born poet, was one of the most wide-ranging and influential of his generation.

It is almost the definition of a Christian that he is somebody who *knows* he isn't one, either in faith or morals. Where faith is concerned, very few of us have the right to say more than – to vary a saying of Simone Weil's – 'I believe in a God who is like the True God in everything except that he does not exist, for I have not yet reached the point where God exists.' As for loving and forgiving our enemies, the less we say about that the better. Our lack of faith and love are facts we have to acknowledge, but we shall not improve either by a morbid and essentially narcissistic moaning over our deficiencies. Let us rather ask, with caution and humour – given our time and place and talents, what, if our faith and love were perfect, would we be glad to find it obvious to do?

(From a sermon)

'What do you think? A man had two sons; he went to the first and said, "Son, go and work in the vineyard today." He answered, "I will not"; but later he changed his mind and went. The father went to the second and said the same; and he answered, "I go, sir"; but he did not go. Which of the two did the will of his father?' (Matthew 21.28–31a)

> God of truth: some of us shout your name,
> confident in our believing and judgemental in our actions;
> some of us play safe and live quiet lives,
> not interfering, not needing to believe or
> to do very much;
> a few of us diffidently keep the door open
> to truth and our neighbour,
> and do not lose sight of the call to love.

ONE WHO IS WISE IS CAUTIOUS IN EVERYTHING. (Sirach 18.27)

MONICA BALDWIN · *Inward urges*

Monica Baldwin (b.1896) spent many years as a nun before, with some difficulty, leaving her order. She wrote about her experiences in I Leap over the Wall *and, fictionally, in* The Called and the Chosen.

In reviewing my misspent life, I am increasingly impressed by the fact that all my worst mistakes have resulted from turning a deaf ear to Inward Urges.

I say 'urge' rather than 'inspiration', because an Urge is such a queer, inexplicable thing that one hesitates to think of it as strictly spiritual. Indeed, in my case, Urges usually begin to operate from a prosaic spot somewhere in the pit of the stomach. Like some blind, irresistible force, they take complete possession of one's being, impelling one to follow or to refrain from, some particular course of action. Should one, however, struggle to resist, and continue resisting, the Urge gradually fades out and ends by disappearing altogether. When this happens, I have observed that the remembrance of it tends to haunt one uncomfortably in the years that follow.

All my life I have been subject to these Urges. Now and again, I have revisited them in order to follow what then sounded like excellent advice. I have invariably regretted it. When, however, I have obeyed my Urge, no matter how crazy the course of action may have seemed at the moment, it has always turned out for the best.

(*I Leap over the Wall*)

[Wisdom speaks:]
Happy is the one who listens to me,
    watching daily at my gates,
    waiting beside my doors.
For whoever finds me finds life.
(Proverbs 8.34–5)

        Holy Wisdom,
        may I wait
        for your quietness
        to speak.

LEAP BEFORE YOU LOOK. (W. H. Auden, title of poem)

BASIL OF CAESAREA · *Letter-writing*

Basil of Caesarea (c.329–79) was one of the greatest of the Greek-speaking Church Fathers, a weighty thinker about the central mysteries of the Christian faith. As bishop of his home-town he was an able defender of the faith – and a man who needed and valued his friends.

Once upon a time you used to send me brief notes – now I do not get even that from you. This economy with words, if it carries on, will lead to total speechlessness. Please, please return to your old ways: I will never tease you for your Spartan letters again. Even a little note will be taken as a sign of great goodwill and valued accordingly. Only do write!

PS Everything has its proper season: spring for flowers, summer for the sprouting ears of wheat, autumn for apples – and winter's produce is conversation!

(Letters XII and XIII to Olympius)

I have written this short letter to encourage you, and to testify that this is the true grace of God. Stand fast in it. Your sister church in Babylon, chosen together with you, sends you greetings; and so does my son Mark. Greet one another with a kiss of love. (1 Peter 5.12–14)

> May my tongue cleave to the roof of my mouth
> if I forget to speak with my friends.

I HAVE MADE THIS LETTER LONGER THAN USUAL, ONLY BECAUSE I HAVE NOT HAD TIME TO MAKE IT SHORTER. (Blaise Pascal)

RICHARD BAXTER · *Wise ignorance*

Richard Baxter (1615–91) was an English Nonconformist clergyman, driven out of the Church of England by the Act of Uniformity of 1662. Towards the end of his life he was tried before the notorious Judge Jeffreys and imprisoned for eighteen months.

Heretofore I knew much less than now, and yet was not half so much acquainted with my ignorance. I had a great delight in the daily new discoveries which I made, and of the light which shined in upon me (like a man that cometh into a country where he never was before); but I little knew either how imperfectly I understood these very points whose discovery so delighted me, nor how much might be said against them, nor how many things I was yet a stranger to. But now I find far greater darkness upon all things, and perceive how very little it is that we know in comparison with that which we are ignorant of, and have far meaner thoughts of my own understanding, though I must needs know that it is better furnished than it was then.

(From his autobiography)

When I was a child, I spoke like a child, I thought like a child, I reasoned like a child; when I became an adult, I put an end to childish ways. For now we see in a mirror, dimly, but then we will see face to face. Now I know only in part; then I will know fully, even as I have been fully known. (1 Corinthians 13.11–12)

> God of all ages,
> may we not altogether lose the open-eyed wonder
>   of children,
> but eagerly let go of all that may cloud the vision
> of your infinite loving.

THERE IS A LOT TO BE SAID ... FOR BELIEVING MORE AND MORE IN LESS AND LESS. (John Yates)

AGNES BEAUMONT · *Help in trouble*

Agnes Beaumont (1652–1720) was a member of John Bunyan's congregation in Bedford from 1672, against the will of her father. Her father became ill and died, and an ill-wisher accused Agnes of his murder.

I see that to be brought before a company of men, and to come before them accused of murdering my own father, that, although I knew myself clear in the sight of God, yet without abundance of his presence, I should sink before them. I thought, if they should see me dejected and looking daunted, they would think I was guilty. I begged of the Lord that he would be pleased to carry me above the fears of men, and devils, and death itself; and that he would give me faith and courage that I might look my accuser in the face with boldness ... And as I was earnestly crying to the Lord, with many tears, for his presence, that blessed word darted in upon my mind: 'The righteous shall hold on their way, and they that have clean hands shall grow stronger and stronger.' ... I thought it was such a suitable word, I could scarce have had the like; and the Lord made it good ere the sun went down, every bit of it.

(*The Narrative of the Persecution of Agnes Beaumont in 1674*)

But you, gird your loins; stand up and tell them everything that I command you. Do not break down before them, or I will break you before them. And I for my part have made you today a fortified city, an iron pillar, and a bronze wall, against the whole land ... They will fight against you; but they shall not prevail against you, for I am with you says the Lord, to deliver you. (Jeremiah 1.17–19)

Just God, I do not know whether to praise you more for giving one person, faced with evil, a flinty countenance, or for giving another, in the same danger, the grace of serene dignity. I only ask you, give us all the courage to be true to the selves you created us to become.

I HAVE NEVER LIKED YOUR MANNER TOWARD ME BETTER THAN WHEN YOU KISSED ME LAST FOR I LOVE WHEN DAUGHTERLY LOVE AND DEAR CHARITY HATH NO LEISURE TO LOOK TO WORLDLY COURTESY. (Thomas More, to his daughter, the day before his execution)

7

JULIA DE BEAUSOBRE · *Creative suffering*

Julia de Beausobre (1894–1977), of aristocratic Russian birth, underwent imprisonment, solitary confinement, interrogation and sickness, and experienced life in a concentration camp in Soviet Russia, before being ransomed by her former English governess and beginning her life in England. Her son and husband had died in Russia.

The other way of coping with sadism is very hard. It is pre-eminently active. It exacts of the victim who undertakes it a heightening of consciousness, which is inseparable from the pain that goes with any expansion of awareness. It demands simultaneous participation, by an intense effort of sympathetic insight, in the particular and the general context of the action; insight into the entirety of your present situation; ... penetration, as far as possible, into the minds of those who have staged the 'cross-examination', and insight into the breadth of God's composition for this particular event on earth ... All this is very hard. But the point is that once it is achieved, you realize that you have been privileged to take part in nothing less than an act of redemption ... This ... way of meeting such an evil ... takes it for granted that any and every deed of ugliness can and should be redeemed and transfigured, and that, in all ordinary circumstances, [one] must participate in the deed done, [in order] to participate in its redemption.

(Creative Suffering)

On that day Israel will be the third with Egypt and Assyria, a blessing in the midst of the earth, whom the Lord of hosts has blessed, saying, 'Blessed be Egypt my people, and Assyria the work of my hands, and Israel my heritage.' (Isaiah 19.24)

> Let us not forget, God,
> that with you nothing is impossible,
> and that your redeeming love knows no limits,
> even though we ourselves may be its agents.

ONLY GRACE CAN BE FREE WITHOUT BEING CHEAP. (Anonymous)

BENEDICT OF NURSIA · *Community life*

Benedict (c.480–c.547), the 'father of western monasticism', was abbot of Monte Cassino in Italy.

The cellarer should not annoy the members [that is, of the monastic community]. If anyone happens to make an unreasonable demand, the cellarer should not reject that person with disdain and cause distress, but reasonably and humbly deny the improper request.

(Rule of St Benedict)

On the third day Joseph said to [his brothers], 'Do this and you will live, for I fear God: if you are honest men, let one of your brothers stay here where you are imprisoned. The rest of you shall go and carry grain for the famine of your households, and bring your youngest brother to me. Thus your words will be verified, and you shall not die.' (Genesis 42.18–20)

> When I ought to say No,
> let me say it simply.
> When I need to say No,
> let me say it courteously.
> When I want to say No,
> let me weigh my words carefully.

YOU KNOW WHAT CHARM IS: A WAY OF GETTING THE ANSWER YES WITHOUT HAVING ASKED ANY CLEAR QUESTION. (Albert Camus)

KATHLEEN BLISS · *Language*

Kathleen Bliss (1908–89) studied history and theology at Cambridge. She travelled widely, and organized debates between Christians, humanists and others for the BBC. As well as teaching and broadcasting, she was general secretary of the Church of England Board of Education, and was associated for twenty years with the World Council of Churches.

If language is a creative faculty, then we have to use it boldly to describe for ourselves and others whatever has the ring of truth and genuineness for us ... If we are open to the possibilities of language we will be sensitive to the use of it by others and recognize that others may be speaking of profoundly religious matters without using traditional language.

(The Future of Religion)

The good person out of the good treasure of the heart produces good, and the evil person out of evil treasure produces evil; for it is out of the abundance of the heart that the mouth speaks. (Luke 6.45)

> May we
> hear the truth,
> speak the truth,
> live the truth.

GOD MADE US WITH TWO EARS AND ONLY ONE MOUTH.
(Rabbinic saying)

DIETRICH BONHOEFFER · *Absence*

Dietrich Bonhoeffer (1906–45) was a German Lutheran pastor and theologian whose work was influenced by the Swiss theologian Karl Barth. He was a strong opponent of National Socialism (i.e. Nazism) and became deeply involved in the German resistance movement. He was arrested and imprisoned in 1943, and hanged in 1945.

Nothing can make up for the absence of someone whom we love, and it would be wrong to try to find a substitute; we must simply hold out and see it through. That sounds very hard at first, but at the same time it is a great consolation, for the gap, as long as it remains unfilled, preserves the bonds between us. It is nonsense to say that God fills the gap; he doesn't fill it, but on the contrary, keeps it empty and so helps us to maintain our former communion with each other even at the cost of pain.

(Letters and Papers from Prison)

When Jesus saw [Mary] weeping, and the Jews who came with her also weeping, he was greatly disturbed in spirit and deeply moved. He said, 'Where have you laid him?' They said to him, 'Lord, come and see.' Jesus began to weep. (John 11.33–5)

> O God, you make us for love
>   and for one another.
> Comfort us in our losses
> and show us that love
>   which is beyond death.

REMEMBER THAT WE MUST ALL DIE. (Ecclesiasticus 8.7)

ELIZABETH BOWEN · *Vision*

Elizabeth Bowen (1899–1973) was an Irish novelist, short-story writer and literary critic.

Throughout [Paul's] discourses, teaching and writings is the stress on vision – as a faculty, in the optic sense. Loss of his sight, for three days, after the blaze of light on the road to Damascus, gave him to know in body what blindness was, to contemplate what in spirit it had amounted to. After that, could he forget the miracle which caused, instantly, scales to drop from his eyes? Nothing could be the same again. Christianity is a revolutionary insistence upon seeing, seeing anew – it was in that sense that it was a threat to Rome, to the maintenance of observances and conformities which, built into the system, indeed, its build-up, had to be seen in (only) the Roman way ... What aroused mistrust with regard to Christians was not their conduct, against which little could be brought, but their attitude, felt to be subversive.

(*A Time in Rome*)

Tobias went up to him ... saying, 'Take courage, father.' With this he applied the medicine on his eyes, and ... peeled off the white films from the corners of his eyes. Then Tobit saw his son and ... said, 'I see you, my son, the light of my eyes!' (from Tobit 11.10–14)

> All-seeing One,
>   do not leave us with our eyes
>   closed to your truth,
>   but open the eyes of peoples
>   that we may see, and turn,
>   and be healed.

BEHOLD I AM DOING A NEW THING ... DO YOU NOT PERCEIVE IT? (Isaiah 43.19 RSV)

MARTIN BUBER · *Relationship*

Martin Buber (1878–1965) was an Austrian Jewish philosopher and theologian. Born in Vienna, he fled to Palestine in 1938 to escape the Nazis, and became professor of social philosophy at Jerusalem. He wrote widely on social and ethical problems.

I consider a tree.

I can look on it as a picture: stiff column in a shock of light, or splash of green shot with the delicate blue and silver of the background.

I can perceive it as movement ...

I can classify it in a species and study it as a type in its structure and mode of life ...

In all this the tree remains my object, occupies space and time, and has its nature and constitution.

It can, however, also come about, if I have both will and grace, that in considering the tree I become bound up in relation to it. The tree is now no longer *It* ...

The tree is no impression, no play of my imagination, no value depending on my mood; but it is bodied over against me and has to do with me, as I with it – only in a different way ... I encounter no soul or dryad of the tree, but the tree itself.

(*I and Thou*)

Jesus stood still ... 'What do you want me to do for you?' ...
'Let me see again.' (Luke 18.40–41)

> Creator God,
> open our eyes to all that is around us.
> Help us to see as you see;
> forgive our shortsightedness.
> Help us to look on your world
> with compassion and a true desire for justice.

'I CAN SEE PEOPLE, BUT THEY LOOK LIKE TREES, WALKING.' (Mark 8.24)

FANNY BURNEY · *Answer to prayer*

Fanny Burney (1752–1840) was an English novelist and diarist.

The stroke was confined to [Dr Johnson's] tongue. Mrs Williams told me a most striking and touching circumstance that attended the attack. It was about four o'clock in the morning: he found himself with a paralytic affection; he rose, and composed in his own mind a Latin prayer to the Almighty, 'that whatever were the sufferings for which he must prepare himself, it would please Him, through the grace and mediation of our blessed Saviour, to spare his intellects, and let them all fall upon his body.' When he had composed this, internally, he endeavoured to speak it aloud, but found his voice was gone.

(*The Diary of Fanny Burney*)

I held my tongue, and spake nothing: I kept silence, yea, even from good words; but it was pain and grief to me. (Psalm 39.3, Book of Common Prayer)

> God,
> when our prayers are answered
> with shocking literalness,
> and the joke is on us,
> let us call upon you for
> fresh resources of wisdom
> to stand in face of your judgements
> of terror and love.

How sickness enlarges the dimension of a man's self to himself. (Charles Lamb)

14

JOSEPHINE BUTLER · *Confronting the powerful*

Josephine Butler (1828–1906) was an English social reformer, promoter of women's education and campaigner against licensed brothels, the white-slave trade, and the Contagious Diseases Acts (which demeaned women). She worked in international bodies as well as in the United Kingdom.

We arranged that the petition should be taken to the Castle where the Grand Conseil sits, by a deputation of working women. There was much excitement about this, and I had to put the dear bodies through a rehearsal, but it succeeded well, and attracted attention, being something quite new in Switzerland ... I was glad to see that they looked quite 'women of the people' though with well-washed shining faces and their best bonnets on. One was a remarkably handsome woman with splendid dark eyes full of wit and intelligence, and she had a little black woollen shawl pinned at the neck, *bare* muscular arms, and black woollen gloves on her hands, an interval of handsome bare arm showing between shawl and gloves. It looked so nice! ... In about an hour they all came back to my room. I never saw such radiant faces! They all wanted to speak together to tell me what had passed.

(From a letter)

I led them with cords of human kindness,
 with bands of love.
(Hosea 11.4)

> Praise God for all those
> who give voice to the voiceless,
> not just by speaking for them
> but by enabling them to speak for themselves.

It is hard to help people grow up, without treating them like children. (Anonymous)

AMY CARMICHAEL · *Presence*

Amy Carmichael (1867–1951), born in County Down, was a lifelong Protestant missionary, first in Japan but most notably in India.

[In the words of her biographer:] Once [during her last, long illness] she had a vivid dream that she was healed. She walked three miles rejoicing in her strength, and then, when she began to tire a little, she saw a taxi pass. It stopped, but she hesitated, not sure if she had enough money for the fare. But the man said, 'Don't spoil my joy', and so he drove her home. She told him how she had been healed by the touch of the Lord. 'I had such a happy time with him.' But she awoke, and it was a dream.

[Amy wrote:] Sleepless from midnight till about 4 a.m. Woke feeling like ashes – as dull, as grey, in spirit – and all one ache in body. But
To God thanks be
For cups of tea
And APC[1]
And above all for His Presence in the bush. O Lord my God, Thou art my Flame of Fire.

[1] A patent medicine – a compound of aspirin, phenacetin and caffeine.

My desire is to depart and be with Christ, for that is far better; but to remain in the flesh is more necessary for you.
(Philippians 1.23–4)

> When the white heat of activity fades
> and human energies are burned out,
> let your invisible light and warmth
> remain
> protected
> under the ashes.

THE INTERPRETATION OF DREAMS IS THE ROYAL ROAD TO A KNOWLEDGE OF THE UNCONSCIOUS ACTIVITIES OF THE MIND. (Sigmund Freud)

CARLO CARRETTO · *The poverty of wealth*

Carlo Carretto (1910-88) was a Little Brother of the Gospel, well known for his books on spirituality. He spent much of his life either in his order's house in the Sahara or living as a hermit in Umbria (Italy). In later life he directed a centre near Assisi, based on the spirituality of Charles de Foucauld.

We know nothing, or practically nothing, about our eternal destiny, and we cling so tenaciously to what we believe is for our good. Affluent and overfed ourselves, we think that the only evil in the world is hunger; because we get upset by pain and privation, we think that the only problem to be resolved is that of providing bread and better hygienic conditions for the Third World. Of course there are serious problems for which solutions must be found, but what we fail to recognize is the far greater wretchedness of some rich people who die of boredom and drugs in comfortable bourgeois houses, and who stifle their personalities beneath their accumulated wealth and their self-centredness.

What we lack is true perspective, and this distorts the whole picture of our lives.

(In Search of the Beyond)

'But woe to you who are rich,
    for you have received your consolation.
Woe to you who are full now,
    for you will be hungry.'
(Luke 6.24–5)

> God, forgive my arrogance.
> Give me knowledge of my poverty,
> and if I can't see as others see,
> then make me listen to their prophets.

WAKEFULNESS OVER WEALTH WASTES AWAY ONE'S FLESH.
(Sirach 31.1)

VIRGINIA CARVER · *Water*

Virginia Carver (1918–74) was a member of the Community of St Clare, an Anglican contemplative community.

Take just this one thing, water. How in fact has it disclosed its meaning to us? In the beginning there were many things. There was the bath, the shock of immersion in water, fierce taps with hot water that scalds, cold water that bites, and the mysterious, living waste pipe that sucks at your foot, seizes and drags at the flannel, snarls and gurgles as it devours the bath water. There is the ritual of washing. A good mother provides a good ritual; always washes in the same order, always the same words, the same horror at the dirt before scrubbing, the same wonder at the cleanliness after; and after washing a ritual time allowed for splash and wallow and fun with sponges. A good mother provides a good lap for drying, and a ritual rub with a clean towel.

(The Great Shift)

For thus says the Lord:
I will extend prosperity to her like a river,
   and the wealth of the nations like an overflowing
     stream;
and you shall nurse and be carried on her arm,
   and dandled on her knees.
As a mother comforts her child,
   so I will comfort you;
   you shall be comforted in Jerusalem.
You shall see, and your heart shall rejoice;
   your bodies shall flourish like the grass.
(Isaiah 66.12–14)

> May we pray and work for a world
> where mothers have time to enjoy their children,
> where children grow up with happy memories,
> and where all the rituals of life are
> transformed by our recognition
> of your presence.

WATER IS BEST. (Pindar)

IRENE CLAREMONT DE CASTILLEJO ·
Integrity

Irene Claremont de Castillejo (b. 1896) was a noted Jungian psychologist.

One of the main reasons why we so often fail to meet other people is that we are so seldom really there.

To begin with we are so often identified with our roles in society, and no one can meet a role. I cannot meet a doctor, a civil servant, a hospital nurse, or a shop girl unless these throw off their disguise and look me in the eye – any more than I can meet an acted Hamlet, though I might conceivably meet a real one. Similarly, to be met I must be myself.

(Knowing Woman)

So Pharaoh called Abram, and said, 'What is this you have done to me? Why did you not tell me she was your wife? Why did you say, "She is my sister", so that I took her for my wife? Now then, here is your wife, take her, and be gone.' (Genesis 12.18–19)

> God, forgive us our need
> to shelter behind roles
> (boss, expert, parent, child),
> and teach us
> how to be ourselves,
> in our roles and out of them.

No mask like open truth to cover lies, As to go naked is the best disguise. (William Congreve)

ELIZABETH CATEZ · *Not knowing*

Elizabeth Catez (1880–1906) was a Carmelite of Dijon (Sister Elizabeth of the Trinity). In her, the 'not-knowing', characteristic of the Carmelite way, found expression in a trinitarian spirituality which was both traditionally orthodox and peculiarly her own.

'*Nescivi!* – I knew not.'[1] So sings the Bride of the Canticle after having been brought into the inner cellar. That, it seems to me, should also be the song of a 'Praise of Glory'[2] on the first day of her retreat, when the Master makes her sound the depths of the bottomless abyss, that she may learn to fulfil the office which will be hers in eternity and which she also ought to perform in time, which is eternity begun and ever in progress.

('The last retreat of *Laudem Gloriae*')

[1] Song of Solomon 6.12 (not in all English versions).
[2] 'Praise of Glory' (Latin, *Laudem Gloriae*), Sister Elizabeth's name for herself – see Ephesians 1.12.

'No eye has seen, nor ear heard,
   nor the human heart conceived,
what God has prepared for those who love him.'
(1 Corinthians 2.9, possibly conflating passages from the Hebrew Testament)

> Love unknown,
> let all the earth fall silent
> to make room
> for you.

WE DON'T NEED RELIGION TO HELP US *KNOW* AT THE MOMENT; WE NEED IT TO HELP US STAY WITH THE 'I DON'T KNOW' IN OUR LIVES. (Hannah Ward)

p.3 W H Auden.

Yes I agree, but what of those who are so sure
How sure was Jesus? Tempted - Forsaken?
"would we be glad to find it obvious to do?" What does he mean
Even those of us who doubt - judge.

p 6 Richard Buster

The more you know the more you know
you don't know

CLARE OF ASSISI · *Seeing in a mirror*

Clare of Assisi (1194–1253) was founder of the Poor Clares and friend of St Francis.

Place your mind before the mirror of eternity!
Place your soul in the brilliance of glory!
Place your heart in the figure of the divine substance!
And transform your whole being into the image of the Godhead
    Itself through contemplation!
                    (From the third letter to Blessed Agnes of Prague)

And all of us, with unveiled faces, seeing the glory of the Lord
as though reflected in a mirror, are being transformed into the
same image from one degree of glory to another.
(2 Corinthians 3.18)

> Blessing you, may we be blessed;
> glorifying you, may we behold your glory;
> reflecting on you, may we reflect your true image;
> being made like you, may we see you as you are.

FOR NOW WE SEE IN A MIRROR, DIMLY, BUT THEN WE WILL SEE FACE
TO FACE. (1 Corinthians 13.12)

HANNAH CULLWICK · *All in a day's work*

Hannah Cullwick (1833–1909), born in Shropshire, was a domestic servant for most of her life.

This is the beginning of another year, & I am still general servant like, to Mrs Henderson at 20 Gloucester Crescent. This month on the 16th I shall o' bin in her service 2 years & a ½, & if I live till the 26th o' May when I shall be 38 year old, I shall o' bin in service 30 years . . . I clean all the copper scuttles & dig the coals, clean the tins & help to clean the silver & do the washing up if I'm wanted, & carry things up as far as the door for dinner. I clean 4 grates & do the fires & clean the irons, sweep & clean 3 rooms & my attic, the hall & front steps & the flags & the area railings & all that in the street. I clean the water closet & privy out & the backyard & the area, the back stairs & the passage, the larder pantry & boy's room & the kitchen & scullery, all the cupboards downstairs & them in the storeroom.

(Diary entry for 1 January 1871)

'Who among you would say to your slave who has just come in from ploughing or tending sheep in the field, "Come here at once and take your place at the table"? Would you not rather say to him, "Prepare supper for me, put on your apron and serve me while I eat and drink; later you may eat and drink"? Do you thank the slave for doing what was commanded? So you also, when you have done all that you were ordered to do, say, "We are worthless slaves; we have done only what we ought to have done!" ' (Luke 17.7–10)

> God our host,
> some of those who in this life
> have not been allowed so much as to serve at their
>   masters' table,
> have sat down in your presence,
> eating and drinking at your heavenly feast.

AVERAGE YEARLY WAGES FOR THE MAID-OF-ALL-WORK IN ABOUT 1860, ACCORDING TO MRS BEETON, WAS £9 TO £14 A YEAR – REDUCED IF SOME FOOD ALLOWANCE WAS MADE.

ELIZABETH DAVID · *Bread*

Elizabeth David (1913–92), English writer on food and cookery, brought new life to British cookery in the years after World War II.

The interdependence between the grain and the yeast, between bread and fermenting liquor, was certainly established ... in the earliest times and has persisted throughout history. This circumstance, together with its very mystery, accounts perhaps for the curiously ambivalent attitude towards leavened bread and leaven generally as expressed in both the Old Testament and the New; 'a symbol of silent pervasive influence, usually of that which is corrupt', my Concordance explains. We know that St Paul used it as a figure of speech signifying corruption ... In Chaucer's England one of the names for yeast or barm was goddisgoode 'bicause it cometh of the grete grace of God'. These words imply a blessing. To me that is just what it is. It is also mysterious, magical. No matter how familiar its action may become nor how successful the attempts to explain it in terms of chemistry and to manufacture it by the ton, yeast still to a certain extent retains its mystery.

(English Bread and Yeast Cookery)

Your boasting is not a good thing. Do you not know that a little yeast leavens the whole batch of dough? Clean out the old yeast that you may be a new batch, as you really are unleavened. For our paschal lamb, Christ, has been sacrificed. Therefore, let us celebrate the festival, not with the old yeast, the yeast of malice and evil, but with the unleavened bread of sincerity and truth. (1 Corinthians 5.6–8)

> For the bread we eat and
> the life we are given by it –
> Thanks be to God.

AND AGAIN HE SAID, 'TO WHAT SHALL I COMPARE THE KINGDOM OF GOD? IT IS LIKE YEAST THAT A WOMAN TOOK AND MIXED IN WITH THREE MEASURES OF FLOUR UNTIL ALL OF IT WAS LEAVENED.' (Luke 13.20)

JOY DAVIDMAN · *Seen from outside*

Joy Davidman (1915–60), poet, novelist and writer, was born in New York, eventually moved to England with the two sons of her first marriage, and in 1957 married C. S. Lewis.

[From a Martian's aerial observations of life in the USA on a sunny Sunday:]

There exists, however, a small sect of recalcitrants or heretics that does not practise sun worship. These may be identified by their habit of clothing themselves more soberly and completely than the sun worshippers. They too gather in groups, but only to hide from the sun in certain buildings of doubtful use, usually with windows of glass coloured to keep out the light. It is not clear whether these creatures are simply unbelievers or whether they are excommunicated from sun worship for some offence – we have not been able to discover what goes on within their buildings, which may perhaps be places of punishment. But it is noteworthy that their faces and gestures show none of the almost orgiastic religious frenzy with which the sun worshippers pursue their devotions. In fact, they usually appear relaxed and even placid, thus indicating minds blank of thought or emotion.

(*Smoke on the Mountain*)

'Athenians, I see how extremely religious you are in every way.' (Acts 17.22)

> Dear God,
> may we never cease to learn
> from the contempt of our critics
> and the laughter of our friends;
> and may we bring to your worship
> all that we have,
> all that we are,
> and eagerly await
> your transforming touch.

O wad some Pow'r the giftie gie us To see oursels as others see us! (Robert Burns)

EMILY DICKINSON · *Bereavement*

Emily Dickinson (1830–86), American poet, spent her whole life in Amherst, Massachusetts, where from the age of 23 she lived an intensely secluded life, secretly writing over a thousand poems, almost all of which remained unpublished till after her death.

Dear Friend, I think of you so wholly that I cannot resist to write again, to ask if you are safe?

Danger is not at first, for then we are unconscious, but in the after, slower, days.

Do not try to be saved, but let Redemption find you, as it certainly will.

Love is its own rescue, for we, at our supremest, are but its trembling Emblems.

(From a letter to a friend on his wife's death)

'The kingdom of God is as when a farmer scatters seed on the ground, and sleeps and wakes up day after day, and the seed sprouts and grows, without the farmer knowing how.'
(Mark 4.26–7, compilers' translation)

> We ask
> for minds open to wonder,
> for endurance to wait for the right moment,
> for eyes and ears alert to recognize your presence,
> for hearts enlarged to receive your gift –
> yourself, our God.

ALL THEORY IS GREY, DEAR FRIEND, BUT GREEN IS THE GOLDEN TREE.
(Goethe)

C. H. DODD · *True prayer*

Charles Harold Dodd (1884–1973) was a Congregational minister, and one of the most notable biblical scholars of his time.

Christ's 'journeying' to the Father is neither a physical movement in space, such as a bodily ascension to heaven, nor is it the physical act of dying. It is that spiritual ascent to God which is the inward reality of all true prayer. And this ascent in prayer carries with it all those who are included in the intercession which is, again, inseparable from all true prayer. In thus praying, Christ both accomplishes the self-oblation of which his death is the historical expression, and 'draws' all [people] after him into the sphere of eternal life which is union with God.

(*The Interpretation of the Fourth Gospel*)

Happy are those whose strength is in you,
   in whose heart are the highways to Zion.
(Psalm 84.5)

> Jesus,
>   let us walk with you to God;
>   let us stand with you before God;
>   let us live with you in God;
>   let us love with you from God.

TO BEAR FRUIT UPWARDS WE MUST TAKE ROOT DOWNWARDS.
(see 2 Kings 19.30)

CATHERINE DE HUECK DOHERTY ·
Foggy days

Catherine de Hueck Doherty (1896–1985), born in Russia, experienced both wealth and poverty in Canada and the USA, before going to live, at first in solitude, on an island jutting out into the Madawaska River in Ontario, Canada. Her island became a centre of prayer for the community she founded. She continues to inspire many through her writings.

A fog surrounds my island today. It is one of those strange, somewhat mysteriously depressing days that come to our mountains. It makes the rivers and lakes and everything look out of proportion. I call them my days of temptations. Fog distorts, and distortions confuse and even frighten one. Therefore, my companions on a foggy day like this seem, for a while, to be Confusion, Chaos, Distortion and Fear.

(Welcome, Pilgrim)

When he utters his voice, there is a tumult of waters
    in the heavens,
  and he makes the mist rise from the ends of the
    earth.
(Jeremiah 10.13)

> How long, O Lord,
> will you hide your face from me?
> Let the clouds depart;
> let the heavens declare your glory.

THE WEATHER IS ALWAYS DOING SOMETHING THERE. (Mark Twain)

JOHN DONNE · *Expectation*

John Donne (c.1572–1631) was an English poet and (from 1614) an Anglican clergyman, later Dean of St Paul's. His life was a mixture of ambition and anguish, his hopes for a successful career in public life being blighted by his clandestine marriage to his employer's niece.

The ends crowne our workes, but thou crown'st our ends,
For, at our end begins our endless rest;
The first last end, now zealously possest,
With a strong sober thirst, my soule attends.
'Tis time that heart and voice be lifted high,
Salvation to all that will is nigh.

(*Holy Sonnets*, 'La Corona')

As a deer longs for flowing streams,
    so my soul longs for you, O God.
My soul thirsts for God,
    for the living God.
When shall I come and behold
    the face of God? ...
Hope in God; for I shall again praise him,
    my help and my God.
(Psalm 42.1–2, 11)

You alone are our rest and
you are at hand
to free us from our miserable errors
and set us on your own path;
you comfort us and tell us:
'Go confidently
for I myself will carry you
to your journey's end,
and there too I will carry you.'
(based on Augustine)

[MARRIAGE] IS, OF ALL TRANSACTIONS, THE ONE IN WHICH PEOPLE
EXPECT MOST FROM OTHERS, AND ARE LEAST HONEST THEMSELVES.
(Jane Austen)

ANTOINETTE DOOLITTLE · *Prophets*

Shaker Eldress Antoinette Doolittle was a leader, with Elder Frederick Evans, at the North Family community of the Mt Lebanon Shaker settlement in New York state, in the nineteenth century.

Every cycle has its prophets – as guiding stars; and they are the burning candles of the Lord to light the spiritual temple on earth, for the time being. When they have done their work, they will pass away; but the candlesticks will remain, and other lights will be placed in them.

(The Shaker II, 1872, 6, p. 42)

For everything there is a season, and a time for every matter under heaven:
　　a time to be born, and a time to die;
　　a time to plant, and a time to pluck up what is planted;
　　a time to kill, and a time to heal;
　　a time to break down, and a time to build up.
(Ecclesiastes 3.1–3)

> Light of the world,
> in your light may we see light
> and honour your prophets,
> and when prophecy is silent
> let us listen and look
> for the light of your word.

LET GO, AND LET GOD. (Alcoholics Anonymous slogan)

AUSTIN FARRER · *God's will*

Austin Farrer (1906–68) was an Anglican priest and theologian, a gifted preacher and an original thinker and biblical scholar.

We are not to think of God's will as a shy secret hidden somewhere under the root of our mind, and there to be dived for. God's will is written across the face of the world ... The God of religion is not different from the God of rational inquiry. To see into the active cause of the world is to find a sovereign and creative will; and that is the will which religion embraces. Not indeed that the pious Christian is called upon to become God's instrument in shaping the heavens, or in the evolution of species still unborn and unthought. The divine will touches us in that detail of the whole design which involves us.

(A Science of God?)

Thus says God, the Lord,
   who created the heavens and stretched them out,
   who spread out the earth and what comes from it,
who gives breath to the people upon it
   and spirit to those who walk in it:
I am the Lord, I have called you in righteousness,
   I have taken you by the hand and kept you.
(Isaiah 42.5–6)

> Maker of all,
> let us not
> through misplaced modesty
> or indolence
> shirk our role
> in your making.

As for Doing-good, that is one of the professions which are full. (Henry David Thoreau)

GEORGE FOX · *Pure religion*

George Fox (1624–91), religious leader and founder of the Society of Friends (Quakers), was a rebel against formalism in religion, and was deeply shocked by the failure of Christians to live up to their profession.

How are you in the pure Religion, to visit the sick, the fatherless, and the widows, when both blind, and sick, and halt and lame lie up and down, cry up and down almost in every corner of the city, and men and women are so decked with gold and silver in their delicate state, that they cannot tell how to go? Surely, surely you know not that you are all of one mould and blood, that dwell upon the face of the earth. Would not a little out of your abundance and superfluity maintain these poor children, halt, lame, and blind, or set them at work that can work and they that cannot, find a place of relief for them; would not that be a grace to you?

(*Doctrinals to Magistrates*, 1657)

Is not this the fast that I choose:
   to loose the bonds of injustice,
   to undo the thongs of the yoke,
to let the oppressed go free,
   and to break every yoke?
(Isaiah 58.6)

> God of judgement and justice,
> we stand before you as those
> who allow our politicians to count it a virtue
> not to add a penny to our tax so as
> better to house the poor among us
> or to set free the nations of the world that are
> deep in debt to us.
>
> Overflow into action our shame before them and
> before you.

ELIZABETH FRY · *Mysterious God*

Elizabeth Fry (1780–1845), the great Quaker prison reformer, was born near Norwich.

I do not know the course I am to run, all is hid in mystery, but I try to do right in everything ... Look up to true religion as the very first of blessings, cherish it, nourish and let it flourish and bloom in my heart; it wants taking care of, it is difficult to obtain. I must not despair or grow sceptical if I do not always feel religious. I felt God as it were, and I must seek to find [God] again.

(Memoir of the Life of Elizabeth Fry)

Do not winnow in every wind,
 or follow every path.
Stand firm for what you know.
(Sirach 5.9)

> God of the future,
> help us to live with
> what we do not know.

WITHOUT ANY DOUBT, THE MYSTERY OF OUR RELIGION IS GREAT.
(1 Timothy 3.16)

IDA FRIEDERIKE GÖRRES · *Sparks of life*

Ida Friederike Görres (b.1901), the daughter of an Austro-Hungarian count and his Japanese wife, has been described as 'one of the foremost Catholic writers and thinkers of modern Germany'. She was a notably honest and independent questioner of accepted ideas and majority views, perhaps best known to English readers for The Hidden Face, *her study of St Thérèse of Lisieux.*

Solace of Pentecost: the recognition (truism, as usual!) that God sees the countless tiny glow-worms in multitudes of us, in spite of everything being as it is, far more than one thinks: the countless hidden soul-sparks in good and in wicked people, in the pious and the others, in the smug and the 'awakened' – insufferable as we all are, good and bad, deep down below it all flickers the tiny flame, ever-turning to HIM, tiny, helpless, but none the less true. And this minute glow-worm dance in the midst of the darkness of the world may well mark out before the angels the outline of the heavenly Jerusalem.

(Broken Lights)

The true light, which enlightens everyone, was coming into the world. (John 1.9)

> Life-giver,
> may we recognize
> the spark of your life
> in all our fellow-creatures,
> and love it into the bright day
> of hearts open to you.

EVEN THE DARKNESS IS NOT DARK TO YOU. (Psalm 139.12)

CAROLINE GRAVESON · *Beauty*

Caroline Graveson was a Quaker, who gave the Swarthmore lecture on 'Religion and Culture' in 1937. She was vice-principal of the women's part of Goldsmith's College, London, for 30 years, and wrote educational books and children's stories.

There is a daily round for beauty as well as for goodness, a world of flowers and books and cinemas and clothes and manners, as well as of mountains and masterpieces. God is in all beauty, not only in the natural beauty of earth and sky, but in all fitness of language and rhythm, whether it describe a heavenly vision or a street fight, a Hamlet or a Falstaff, a philosophy or a joke; in all fitness of line and colour and shade, whether seen in the Sistine Madonna or a child's knitted frock: in all fitness of sound and beat and measure, whether the result be Bach's Passion music or a nursery jingle. The quantity of God, so to speak, varies in the different examples, but his quality of beauty in fitness remains the same.

(Religion and Culture)

'Consider the lilies of the field, how they grow; they neither toil nor spin, yet I tell you, even Solomon in all his glory was not clothed like one of these.' (Matthew 6.28)

> Glory be to God for every kind of beauty:
> in sound and sight,
> in shape and movement,
> in thought and laughter.

DESPISE NOT THESE LITTLE ONES. (see Matthew 18.10)

GREGORY OF NYSSA · *Desire*

Gregory (c.330–c.395), brother of Basil of Caesarea and an original thinker and theologian, was made Bishop of Nyssa c.371. At the Council of Constantinople (381) he was an eloquent defender of the Nicene Creed.

So he desires, not the reflection or the mirrored image of God, but God seen face to face. And the divine voice, by refusing, offers him what he desires: a few words which open out into an immense abyss of thought, the magnificence of God fulfilling his desires, but never promising either peace or satiety. For this is the true vision of God; that those who lift their eyes towards him never cease to desire him.

(The Life of Moses)

Moses said, 'Show me your glory, I pray.' And he said, 'I will make all my goodness pass before you, and will proclaim before you the name, "The LORD"; and I will be gracious to whom I will be gracious, and will show mercy on whom I will show mercy. But', he said, 'you cannot see my face; for no one shall see me and live.' (Exodus 33.18–20)

> Big-Enough God,
> Let us not reduce you
> to the level of our experience,
> but extend ourselves
> from the place where we find ourselves,
> towards you, the Unlimited God.
> ['Big-Enough God' is a phrase borrowed from Sara
> Maitland]

PERHAPS IN RETIREMENT ... A QUIETER, NARROWER KIND OF LIFE CAN BE ADOPTED. BOUNDED BY ENGLISH LITERATURE AND THE ANGLICAN CHURCH AND SMALL PLEASURES LIKE SEWING AND CHOOSING DRESS MATERIAL FOR THIS UNCERTAIN SUMMER.
(Barbara Pym)

HADEWIJCH OF BRABANT ·
The ways of love

*Hadewijch of Brabant was a thirteenth-century mystic who lived as a Beguine –
that is, as a member of an informal community of religious women. At the heart
of her writings is a mysticism of love.*

> In the beginning Love enriched me.
> She added to my sensible joy
> And showed me all the winnings.
> Why does she now run away like a vagabond?
> She added to my sensible joy,
> But now I wander in a strange land.

('Love and Reason')

With my whole heart I seek you;
   do not let me stray from your commandments.
(Psalm 119.10)

> Mysterious God,
> you seem to
> lead us and leave us,
> seduce us and abandon us.
> If you must go,
> come back soon.

LOVE NEVER ENDS. (1 Corinthians 13.8)

HILDEGARD OF BINGEN · *Realms unknown*

Hildegard (1098–1179) became a nun and abbess of a community of nuns near Bingen. She was a woman of wide-ranging knowledge and gifts in the spheres of science, music, theology, painting, healing and social criticism.

Lying long in my bed of sickness, in the 1170th year of the Lord's incarnation, I saw – awake in body and spirit – a most beautiful image of womanly form, more peerless in gentleness, most dear in her delights. Her beauty was so great that the human mind could not fathom it, and her height reached from earth as far as heaven. Her face shone with the greatest radiance, and her eye gazed heavenward. She was dressed in the purest white silk, and enfolded by a cloak studded with precious gems – emerald, sapphire and pearls; her sandals were of onyx. Yet her face was covered in dust, her dress was torn on the right side, her cloak had lost its elegant beauty and her sandals were muddied. And she cried out ... 'The foxes have their lairs, and the birds of the sky their nests, but I have no helper or consoler, no staff on which to lean or be supported by.'

(From a letter)

'When I say, "My bed will comfort me,
   my couch will ease my complaint",
then you scare me with dreams
   and terrify me with visions.'
(Job 7.13–14)

> Awesome God, you call us from what is safe;
> guide us and go with us as we let go
> into the terror and joy of realms unknown.

EVERYTHING BEGINS IN MYSTICISM AND ENDS IN POLITICS.
(Charles Péguy)

ETTY HILLESUM · *Harmony*

Etty Hillesum (1915–43) was a Dutch Jew who died in Auschwitz. Her wartime journal was published in English in 1983.

Life and human relationships are full of subtleties. I know that there is nothing absolute or objectively valid, that knowledge must seep into your blood, into yourself, not just into your head, that you must live it, and here I always come back to what one should strive after with all one's might: one must marry one's feelings to one's beliefs and ideas. That is probably the only way to achieve a measure of harmony in one's life.

(From her diary)

'You shall love the Lord your God with all your heart, and with all your soul, and with all your mind.' (Matthew 22.37)

> God, let me know your love
> in every part of my being,
> that the truth I feel,
> I may live.

TODAY IT IS NOT NEARLY ENOUGH MERELY TO BE A SAINT.
(Simone Weil)

MARY HOBHOUSE · *Leaving home*

Mary Hobhouse (1819–64), wife of the first Anglican bishop of Nelson, New Zealand, emigrated from England in 1859 and died in childbirth five years later.

My dearest Harriet

This time of year you may well believe takes me in thought to dear Wells & makes me think with longing of short dark winter days, though we are enjoying the light & warmth of the Red Sea. Every day now as it widens my separation from home deepens the sense of it. I trust the pain of feeling oneself so cut off from actual visible intercourse will be made the means of bringing me closer to dependence on God, & enabling me also to realize the higher & more lasting communion with those I love which is apt to be overlooked whilst one has the daily & hourly pleasure of communication.

(Letter written 'opposite Suez', Sunday 28 December 1859)

'Go from your country and your kindred and your father's house to the land that I will show you.' (Genesis 12.1)

> Dear God,
> my light-box[1] is my comfort in dark days
> but what shall I do
> when the daylight never fades
> into your friendly and familiar darkness?

[1]Those suffering from seasonal affective disorder (SAD) sometimes use a light-box in winter to combat the depression caused by short hours of daylight.

IN GOD IS NO DARKNESS AT ALL. (see 1 John 1.5)

GERARD MANLEY HOPKINS · *Ordinariness*

Gerard Manley Hopkins (1844–89), English poet and Jesuit, was a friend of Robert Bridges, who published the first edition of Hopkins' poems in 1918, nearly 30 years after the poet's death.

St Ignatius himself was certainly, every one who reads his life will allow, one of the most extraordinary men that ever lived; but after the establishment of the Order he lived in Rome so ordinary, so hidden a life, that when after his death they began to move in the process of his canonization one of the Cardinals, who had known him in his later life and in that way only, said that he had never remarked anything in him more than in any edifying priest.

(From a letter to R. W. Dixon, 1 December 1881)

'Is not this the carpenter's son?' (Matthew 13.56)

> Marvellous God,
> never cease to surprise us
> by the way you work in people,
> and by the people who walk with you.

HUMAN BEINGS WORK FROM WITHOUT INWARDS; GOD WORKS FROM WITHIN OUTWARDS. (Jan van Ruysbroeck)

FRIEDRICH VON HÜGEL · *Silence*

Friedrich von Hügel (1852–1925), son of a Scottish mother and an Austrian father, was a Roman Catholic theologian and philosopher who spent most of his adult life in London, though he travelled abroad a great deal. He was a close friend of several of the Roman Catholic 'modernists', though he himself escaped formal condemnation. He became a much respected spiritual guide and counsellor, especially to many outside the Roman Catholic Church.

Be silent about great things – let them grow inside you, never discuss them. Discussion is so limiting and so distracting, it makes things grow smaller. You think you ought to swallow things, when they ought to swallow you. Before all greatness, be silent – in art, in music, in religion, silence.

(*Letters from Baron Friedrich von Hügel to a Niece*)

[Job addressing God:]
'I lay my hand on my mouth.'
(Job 40.4)

> Dear God,
> it has always puzzled me
> that the Bible has so little good to say of silence.
> Is it a paradox of the religion of the Word
> that silence is taken for granted?
> One cannot listen when talking oneself
> but one must listen to hear the right word,
> and hearing, speak it.
> On you alone my soul waits in silence,
> from you comes salvation, comes hope,
> comes everything that is good, is beautiful, is lovely,
> that breaks forth in singing, in beauty.

DON'T CALL THAT SILENCE – THAT WEASEL PACK OF FURTIVE FLYING FANTASIES! (Anonymous)

HARRIET ANN JACOBS · *Betrayal*

Harriet Ann Jacobs (1813–97), born in slavery in North Carolina, after many vicissitudes was purchased by the Colonization Society and freed in 1852. Her book Incidents in the Life of a Slave Girl *was 'edited' by Lydia Maria Child, the abolitionist writer, but the authenticity of her narrative has been established.*

When I was six years old, my mother died; and then, for the first time, I learned, by the talk around me, that I was a slave ... [Later, her kindly 'owner' died, but instead of leaving her free, she bequeathed the young woman to her five-year-old niece.] My mistress had taught me the precepts of God's Word: 'Thou shalt love thy neighbor as thyself.' 'Whatsoever ye would that men should do unto you, do ye even so unto them.' But I was her slave, and I suppose she did not recognize me as her neighbor. I would give much to blot out from my memory that one great wrong. As a child, I loved my mistress; and, looking back on the happy days I spent with her, I try to think with less bitterness of this act of injustice.

(Incidents in the Life of a Slave Girl)

You yourselves recently repented and did what was right in my sight by proclaiming liberty to one another, and you made a covenant before me in the house that is called by my name; but then you turned about and profaned my name when each of you took back your male and female slaves, whom you had set free according to their desire, and you brought them again into subjection. (Jeremiah 34.15–16)

> God of true freedom,
> may we who so easily live
> on the forced labour of others,
> and who so fiercely resent
> any feared diminishment of our rights –
> personal, social or national –
> choose to work with our life's energy
> for the costly freedom of all the redeemed.

THE HURT IS IN THE ACT OF POSSESSION. (Graham Greene)

RICHARD JEFFERIES · *The unquiet heart*

Richard Jefferies (1848–87) was a naturalist and writer whose best-known book, The Story of My Heart, *explored his inner journey and his struggle to express in words both his sense of oneness with the visible world and his longing for its harmony.*

I have only just commenced to realize the immensity of thought which lies outside the knowledge of the senses. Still, on the hills and by the seashore, I seek and pray deeper than ever. The sun burns southwards over the sea and before the wave runs its shadow, constantly slipping on the advancing slope till it curls and covers its dark image at the shore. Over the rim of the horizon waves are flowing as high and wide as those that break upon the beach. These that come to me and beat the trembling shore are like the thoughts that have been known so long; like the ancient, iterated, and reiterated thoughts that have broken on the strand of mind for thousands of years. Beyond and over the horizon I feel that there are other waves of ideas unknown to me, flowing as the stream of ocean flows.

(*The Story of My Heart*)

When he assigned the sea to its limit,
   so that the waters might not transgress his command,
when he marked out the foundations of the earth,
   then I was by him, like a master worker;
and I was daily his delight,
   rejoicing before him always,
rejoicing in his inhabited world
   and delighting in the human race.
(Proverbs 8.29–31)

> Wisdom,
> at your voice silence enfolds the heart
> so that it can forever
> reach out for you who
> forever call from silence to silence,
> from heart to heart.

I KNOW NOTHING, EXCEPT JUST THAT – I KNOW NOTHING. (Socrates)

JEROME · *The perils of preaching*

Jerome (342–420) was the greatest biblical scholar of the early Latin-speaking Church, and translator of the Bible into Latin (the Vulgate version).

Your task as a preacher is to stir your hearers' consciences, not excite roars of applause – their tears are your real claim to glory ... It is bare-faced effrontery for a preacher to try to explain things of which he is ignorant, and then, when he has convinced others, to assume himself that he really knows what he is talking about. My one-time teacher, Gregory of Nazianzus, countered this temptation with wit and elegance: when I asked him to explain the meaning of Luke's phrase ' "secondfirst" Sabbath',[1] he retorted, 'I'll tell you all about that in church – there everyone will applaud what I say and whether you like it or not, you will have to believe you know what you don't know, because if you are the only one silent, everyone else will think you a fool!'

(From Letter 52)

[1] Luke 6.1 – a notoriously obscure expression.

[God] does not regard any who are wise in their own conceit. (Job 37.24)

For Christ [sent me] ... to proclaim the gospel, and not with eloquent wisdom, so that the cross of Christ might not be emptied of its power. (1 Corinthians 1.17)

> Dear God,
> when I meet the all but inevitable temptation
> to meet others' expectations with a show of
>   confidence,
> lay your hand on my sleeve
> to remind me that
> infallibility is always
> a dangerous claim.

[JESUS] REPLIED: 'IF I TELL YOU, YOU WILL NOT BELIEVE; AND IF I QUESTION YOU, YOU WILL NOT ANSWER.' (Luke 22.67–8)

JEROME K. JEROME · *Pain*

Jerome K. Jerome (1859–1927) was an English humorous writer, novelist and playwright. He was born in Staffordshire and brought up in London. His occupations were, successively, clerk, schoolmaster, reporter, actor and journalist.

Sometimes, our pain is very deep and real, and we stand before her very silent, because there is no language for our pain, only a moan. Night's heart is full of pity for us; she cannot ease our aching; she takes our hand in hers, and the little world grows very small and very far beneath us, and, borne on her dark wings, we pass for a moment into a mightier Presence than her own, and in the wondrous light of that great Presence, all human life lies like a book before us, and we know that Pain and Sorrow are but the angels of God.

(Three Men in a Boat)

How long will you hide your face from me?
How long must I bear pain in my soul,
   and have sorrow in my heart all day long?
(Psalm 13.1–2)

> O God,
>   you have shaken my world and split it open;
>   repair the cracks in it, for it totters.
> Hear my cry, O God,
>   and listen to my prayer.

DO NOT PINE AWAY IN THE PAIN OF YOUR WOUNDS, BUT LIVE FROM THE DEPTH OF THEM, MAKING THE EXTENT OF YOUR DESOLATION THE EXTENT OF YOUR REALM. (Charles Williams)

POPE JOHN XXIII · *Right action*

John XXIII (1881–1963) was the Pope who instigated and inspired the Second Vatican Council (1962–5), the outstanding event in the life of the Roman Catholic Church in modern times.

A summary of great graces bestowed on a man who has a low esteem of himself but receives good inspirations and humbly and trustfully proceeds to put them into practice ...

Second grace. To have been able to accept as simple and capable of being immediately put into effect certain ideas which were not in the least complex in themselves, indeed perfectly simple, but far-reaching in their effects and full of responsibilities for the future. I was immediately successful in this, which goes to show that one must accept the good inspirations that come from the Lord, simply and confidently.

(Journal of a Soul)

Little children, let us love, not in word or speech, but in truth and action. And by this we will know that we are from the truth and will reassure our hearts before him whenever our hearts condemn us; for God is greater than our hearts, and he knows everything. Beloved, if our hearts do not condemn us, we have boldness before God; and we receive from him whatever we ask, because we obey his commandments and do what pleases him. (1 John 3.18–22)

> God of all,
> we praise you for those
>   who know the right moment to act;
> may the inspirations of your good Spirit
> find free passage through
>   all your servants.

LITTLE CHILDREN, KEEP YOURSELVES FROM IDOLS. (1 John 5.21)

JOHN THE SOLITARY · *Decisions*

John the Solitary, also known as John of Apamea, is an author whose identity is shrouded in mystery. It is now thought that he lived during the first half of the fifth century, and that his monastery was in the vicinity of Apamea in Syria. 'For John the aim of the Christian life is the actualization, as far as is possible, in this life of the resurrection of Christ, the hope and pledge of which has been given to each Christian at baptism' (Sebastian Brock).

Do not make hard and fast decisions over anything in the future, for you are a created being and your will is subject to changes. Decide in whatever matters you have to reach a decision, but without fixing in your mind that you will not be moved to other things. For it is not by small changes in what you eat that your faithfulness is altered: your service to the Lord of all is performed in the mind, in your inner person; that is where the ministry to Christ takes place.

(Letter to Hesychius)

'It is the Lord our God who brought us ... up from the land of Egypt ... Therefore we also will serve the Lord, for he is our God.' But Joshua said to the people, 'You cannot serve the Lord, for he is a holy God; ... he will not forgive your transgressions or your sins.' ... And the people said to Joshua, 'No, we will serve the Lord!' Then Joshua said to the people, 'You are witnesses against yourselves ...' And they said, 'We are witnesses.' (Joshua 24.17–19, 21–2)

> O God, you have put your mark on us
> and given us your Spirit in our hearts:
> through Jesus, the Yes to all your promises,
> may we say Amen to your glory.

TOMORROW'S LIFE'S TOO LATE; LIVE TODAY. (Martial)

RUFUS JONES · *Religion at home*

Rufus M. Jones (1863–1948) was a North American Quaker, philosopher, and historian of Quakerism.

We never began a day without 'a family gathering' at which mother read a chapter of the Bible, after which there would follow a weighty silence. These silences, during which all the children of our family were hushed with a kind of awe, were very important features of my spiritual development. There was work inside and outside the house waiting to be done, and yet we sat there hushed and quiet, doing nothing. I very quickly discovered that something *real* was taking place. We were feeling our way down to that place from which living words come and very often they did come. Some one would bow and talk with God so simply and quietly that he never seemed far away. The words helped to explain the silence. We were now finding what we had been searching for.

(*Finding the Trail of Life*)

'Happy is the one who listens to me,
   watching daily at my gates,
   waiting beside my doors.
For whoever finds me finds life
   and obtains favour from the Lord.'
(Proverbs 8.34–5)

On you alone, God, we wait in silence,
   from you comes our salvation.
In you we trust at all times,
   with you is our safe shelter,
and our gateway and path
   to the love and service of all.

SILENCE DOES NOT NECESSARILY BROOD OVER A FULL NEST. YOUR STILL FOWL, BLINKING AT YOU WITHOUT REMARK, MAY ALL THE WHILE BE SITTING ON ONE ADDLED EGG. (George Eliot)

HELEN JOSEPH · *House not home*

Helen Joseph (1905–92), English-born, was one of the best known of the women of South Africa who campaigned against apartheid, and was the first person to be placed under house-arrest there.

Weekends were long, even though there was plenty for me to do in my garden. My house had become an empty place and no longer really a home, for a home is the place you share with your family and friends, and this was forbidden. However, the lifting of the actual house-arrest was a victory in itself, even if only for a few months. I think that only when you have lost it, can you know how precious a little freedom can be.

(Side by Side)

'What woman having ten silver coins, if she loses one of them, does not light a lamp, sweep the house, and search carefully until she finds it? When she has found it, she calls together her friends, saying, "Rejoice with me, for I have found the coin that I had lost."' (Luke 15.8–9)

> No one to rejoice with?
> No one to mourn with?
> No one to eat and drink with?
> No one to drop in for a chat over a cup of tea?
> No one to watch growing up?
> No one to sit by dying?
>
> Let our homes be places of sharing,
> and let us keep a sharp eye out
> for the subtle and not so subtle deprivations
> we force on each other.

A HOUSE IS NOT A HOME. (Polly Adler)

JULIAN OF NORWICH · *Indwelling*

Julian of Norwich (c.1342–after 1413) was an English mystic who left an account of the series of visions she had received on 8 May 1373, and a more lengthy meditation on their meaning, made some years later.

We ought to rejoice greatly that God dwells in our soul, and much more greatly ought we to rejoice that our soul dwells in God. Our soul is made to be God's dwelling-place; and the dwelling-place of the soul is God, who is unmade. It is a great insight to see and know within ourselves that God, who is our maker, dwells within us; and an even greater insight to see and know within ourselves that our created soul dwells in the being of God, of whose being we have our own being.

(*A Revelation of Love*)

'Those who love me will keep my word, and my Father will love them, and we will come to them and make our home with them.' (John 14.23)

> Heart and flesh sing for joy to you,
> living God.
> May our songs be united –
> yours in us, the *cantus firmus*, song of creation,
> ours in you, the ever-surprising melodies
> that burst out often in spite of ourselves.
> The point when we hear both – that is insight.

ONE MUST BE GREAT-SOULED INDEED TO MAKE ROOM FOR GOD.
(Anonymous)

KATHY KEAY · *Dry ground*

Kathy Keay (1954–94) was a writer, editor and the founder of the Men, Women and God Trust in the UK.

Turn over
Gently
My dry, cracked soil.
Just a little,
A little at a time.
Let it breathe
In the cooling air of autumn
And then be watered
By Your life-giving rain.

(*Laughter, Silence and Shouting*)

My soul thirsteth for thee, my flesh also longeth after thee: in a barren and dry land where no water is.
(Psalm 63.2, Book of Common Prayer)

When heart and spirit are constrained and bound,
like a good nurse you loose them slowly
lest the shock of release be too great –
a lifeline is just about long enough,
but some of us reach its end earlier
than their friends can easily bear.

LOVE COMFORTETH LIKE SUNSHINE AFTER RAIN.
(William Shakespeare)

SØREN KIERKEGAARD · *Courage*

Søren Kierkegaard (1813–55) was a Danish philosopher and religious thinker, regarded as one of the founders of existentialism. He was a strong critic of the established church in Denmark; he also suffered severe bouts of mental anguish.

Language supplies us with a splendid word, ready to adapt itself in many connections, but never so eagerly as in connection with what is good. It is the word *Courage*. Wherever goodness is, there courage too is found; whatever fate befall the good, courage is still forever on the side of goodness; the good is always courageous, only the evil is cowardly and afraid, and the devil always trembles. This bold word, then, never turning from danger but always facing it, is in itself a proud word; yet how adaptable it is, when we find it sweetly amenable towards every kind of goodness! So is this bold word intolerant of all evil but consistently in harmony with all kinds of goodness.

(Gospel of Sufferings)

Keep alert, stand firm in your faith, be courageous, be strong. Let all that you do be done in love. (1 Corinthians 16.13–14)

> God,
> teach us to use our courage wisely:
> not to waste it, nor deny it,
> not to think we have more than we do.
> May we grow in courage as we come
> to trust ever more in you.

WHENEVER I AM WEAK, THEN I AM STRONG. (2 Corinthians 12.10)

FRANCIS KILVERT · *Revelation*

Francis Kilvert (1840–79) was an English clergyman and diarist. He was a curate at Clyro in Radnorshire, and later Vicar of Bredwardine on the Wye. His Diary (1870–79) gives a vivid picture of rural life in the Welsh Marches.

This afternoon I walked over to Lanhill.

As I came down from the hill into the valley across the golden meadows and along the flower-scented hedges, a great wave of emotion and happiness stirred and rose up within me. I know not why I was so happy, nor what I was expecting, but I was in a delirium of joy, it was one of the supreme moments of existence, a deep delicious draught from the strong, sweet cup of life. It came unsought, unbidden, at the meadow stile, it was one of the flowers of happiness scattered for us and found unexpectedly by the wayside of life. It came silently, suddenly, and it went as it came, but it left a long, lingering glow and glory behind as it faded slowly like a gorgeous sunset, and I shall ever remember the place and the time in which such great happiness fell upon me.

(Diary entry for 24 May 1875)

'The place on which you are standing is holy ground.'
(Exodus 3.5)

I give you thanks, O God, with my whole heart.

EVEN IN LAUGHTER THE HEART IS SAD,
    AND THE END OF JOY IS GRIEF. (Proverbs 14.13)

FRANK LAKE · *Peace, peace?*

Frank Lake (1914–1982), doctor, psychiatrist and missionary, in 1961 founded the Clinical Theology Association, which had a considerable influence on the pastoral training of those in ministry.

The persecution that gives rise to feelings of inferiority, loss of rights, chronic weakness or fatigue, and paranoid feelings, was certainly part of Christ's passivity on the cross. The 'well-being' that was his right, either as Son of God or Son of Man, was extracted from him by stages and nothing at all was put back by way of relief. Betrayed by a friend, denied a proper trial, not allowed to make his defence, outlawed and condemned before the charge was heard, he protests in the name of justice and is struck across the face by a menial court servant. All his rights are taken from him, all his powers of command are superseded.

(*Clinical Theology*)

They have treated the wound of my people
   carelessly,
  saying, 'Peace, peace',
  when there is no peace.
(Jeremiah 6.14)

       God of peace,
       transform our hearts
       and turn our minds
       that we may always and everywhere
       value life more than death.

NON-VIOLENCE IS NO GOOD UNLESS IT IS *EFFECTIVE*. (Simone Weil)

CHARLES LAMB · *Saying grace*

Charles Lamb (1775–1834), English essayist, was born in London. His life was overshadowed by his long guardianship of his sister Mary, who had killed their mother in an attack of the insanity from which she suffered. He had many friends in the literary world, was a gifted literary critic, and one of the great English letter-writers.

The custom of saying grace at meals had, probably, its origin in the early times of the world ... when dinners were precarious things, and a full meal was something more than a common blessing! when a belly-full was a wind-fall, and looked like a special providence ... I own that I am disposed to say grace upon twenty other occasions in the course of the day besides my dinner. I want a form for setting out upon a pleasant walk, for a moonlight ramble, for a friendly meeting, or a solved problem. Why have we none for books, those spiritual repasts – a grace before Milton – a grace before Shakespeare – a devotional exercise proper to be said before reading the *Fairy Queen*?

('Grace before meat')

Let us give thanks, by which we offer to God an acceptable worship with reverence and awe. (Hebrews 12.28)

> God, all-giving,
> may we be open-hearted to receive
> all your gifts with the gratitude that finds
> something in everything
> to marvel over.

GRATITUDE IS THE BEGINNING OF GRACE. (Jerusalem Bible footnote)

LUCY LARCOM · *Moving house*

Lucy Larcom (1824–93), child of a New England family left in poverty by the early death of her father, became a mill-worker, editor, teacher and poet. The family moved to another town so that her mother could run a boarding-house for mill-workers.

To go away from the little garden was almost as bad [as leaving the house]. Its lilacs and peonies were beautiful to me, and in a corner of it was one tiny square of earth that I called my own, where I was at liberty to pull on my pinks and lady's delights every day, to see whether they had taken root, and where I could give my lazy morning-glory seeds a poke, morning after morning, to help them get up and begin their climb. Oh, I should miss the garden very much indeed!

(*A New England Girlhood*)

The Lord God sent [them] forth from the garden of Eden, to till the ground from which they were taken. (Genesis 3.23)

> Dear God,
> do we each need to have our Eden
> so as to lose it but not forget
> the divine goodness and the mystery
> of the processes of our becoming?

A TIME TO PLANT, AND A TIME TO PLUCK UP WHAT IS PLANTED. (Ecclesiastes 3.2)

C. S. LEWIS · *Tested by grief*

Clive Staples Lewis (1898–1963), scholar, writer and Christian apologist, was born in Ulster, and spent most of his working life in Oxford.

Sometimes, Lord, one is tempted to say that if you wanted us to behave like the lilies of the field you might have given us an organization more like theirs. But that, I suppose, is just your grand experiment. Or no ... rather your grand enterprise. To make an organism which is also a spirit; to make that terrible oxymoron, a 'spiritual animal'. To take a poor primate, a beast with nerve-endings all over it, a creature with a stomach that wants to be filled, a breeding animal that wants its mate, and say, 'Now get on with it. Become a god.'

(A Grief Observed)

The crucible is for silver, and the furnace is for gold,
    but the Lord tests the heart.
(Proverbs 17.3)

Maker God,
You have brought me a little bit further than I am ready to go.
Like the small child being coaxed into the sea by its parents,
I have had just about enough for one day.
One day? Enough for one life, I should say.
But when you say 'All right then', and let go my hand
and I head back up the dunes,
your wind blows the sand in my face
and I turn again, torn, and see the light dawning on
those desirable waves.

CRAS INGENS ITERABIMUS AEQUOR.
TOMORROW WE SHALL AGAIN PUT OUT TO SEA. (Horace)

HELEN M. LUKE · *True freedom*

Helen M. Luke (1904–95), a Jungian writer and spiritual guide, was the founder of Apple Farm, a contemplative Jungian community in Three Rivers, Michigan, USA.

Every individual woman who is capable of reflection and discrimination, and who lays claim to freedom, carries a responsibility to ask herself, 'What kind of free spirit is it that breathes through me and is the dominant influence in my life?' To discover this is a task of self-knowledge which demands all the courage, honesty, and perseverance of which we are capable, and we have first to realize that real freedom from servitude comes only when one is capable of freely chosen *service*. We are freed from the *law* by which we have hitherto lived only through the choice of another binding commitment. We may do what we will only when we have learned the nature of love.

(*Woman: Earth and Spirit*)

Be doers of the word, and not merely hearers who deceive themselves. For if any are hearers of the word and not doers, they are like those who look at themselves in a mirror; for they look at themselves and, on going away, immediately forget what they were like. But those who look into the perfect law, the law of liberty, and persevere, being not hearers who forget but doers who act – they will be blessed in their doing. (James 1.22–5)

> By your law you have made us free;
> by your love you have made us free to serve;
> by your life you have freed us
> for life in all its fullness.

LOVE, AND DO WHAT YOU LIKE. (Augustine of Hippo)

JOHN MACMURRAY · *Spirit and matter*

John Macmurray (1891–1976) was a philosopher and Quaker, who, like Martin Buber (see p. 13), 'thought that an isolated self is an unreal abstraction' (John Macquarrie).

Religion is, indeed, spiritual. But the spiritual is not other than the material, but inclusive of it. Spirit is not other than body but more than body. And any effort to establish a spiritual life which is not a material life, any effort to have a religion which does not include and integrate the material aspects of our being, by integrating us with one another in a unity of material life, is an illusion, and a symptom of the immaturity of our religion. Till we have overcome this dualism of Spirit and Matter – not by denying either but by integrating the two in an inseparable wholeness – religion will never know itself or begin its development in maturity. 'Whoso hath this world's goods and seeth his brother have need and shutteth up his bowels of compassion from him, how dwelleth the love of God in him?'

(Reason and Emotion)

I therefore, the prisoner in the Lord, beg you to lead a life worthy of the calling to which you have been called, with all humility and gentleness, with patience, bearing with one another in love, making every effort to maintain the unity of the Spirit in the bond of peace. There is one body and one Spirit, just as you were called to the one hope of your calling, one Lord, one faith, one baptism, one God and Father of all, who is above all and through all and in all. (Ephesians 4.1–6)

> Dear God our Maker,
> since in this world of ours
> body without spirit is dead
> and spirit without body is not human,
> continue your transforming work in us,
> that we may see and love and serve
> in ourselves and each other
> the unifying work of your divine diversity.

IF YOU DON'T EAT, YOU CAN'T PRAY. (Source unknown)

MAKERETI · *Conversation without words*

Makereti (Maggie Papakura) (1872–1939) was a Maori scholar.

A great deal of conversation with relatives or other loved ones is carried on without words, but by gestures, expressions of the face, and by inarticulate sounds. One of the most expressive was an m-sound made with closed lips. This sound had a great variety of meanings, and expressed love and grief, and tenderness and affection. I remember when I returned to New Zealand after many years' absence, my old people did not need to speak to me, but as they looked at me, and uttered this voiceless sound, they expressed all the depth of their love for me.

(The Old-Time Maori)

Joseph made ready his chariot and went up to meet his father Israel in Goshen. He presented himself to him, fell on his neck, and wept on his neck a good while. (Genesis 46.29)

> God, let us not block with words
> the communing that happens best in silence.

THE SPIRIT INTERCEDES WITH SOUNDS TOO DEEP FOR WORDS.
(see Romans 8.26)

MOTHER MARIA · *Worry*

Mother Maria (Lydia Gysi, 1912–77) was born in Basle of a Methodist family, and was received into the Orthodox Church in 1937. In the course of her studies she came to England in 1949, and eventually was allowed to train as an Orthodox nun with the Anglican Benedictine community at West Malling. She remained there for fourteen years, until the opportunity came for her to move to her own monastery, first at Fillgrave, then in the last years of her life, in Yorkshire.

May 1st, 1977

The sun shines brightly at 4 a.m. when worries awake me and then it hides again, when I grow quieter. Always this strangely anguished – over material things – waking up; every morning. It is like a ridiculous sort of passion which tears me limb from limb in the morning. Then gradually I grow calm and reasonable, I mean the grotesque fear leaves me and the grip lets go its grasp. And all this about what I shall soon leave for good – it is strange.

(*Mother Maria: Her Life and Letters*)

You will not fear the terror of the night,
    or the arrow that flies by day,
or the pestilence that stalks in darkness,
    or the destruction that wastes at noonday.
(Psalm 91.5–6)

> But I do fear, my God,
> I do fear.
> Terror possesses me – for a while –
> and then I startle myself
> with calm returning.
> Let me forget neither
> the sharp descent to fear nor
> the free-floating, unsought ascent
> to the light of this world's day.

THE WAY UP AND THE WAY DOWN ARE ONE AND THE SAME.
(Heraclitus)

MOTHER MARIBEL · *Tiredness*

Mother Maribel CSMV (1887–1970) was a member of the Anglican Community of St Mary the Virgin. She trained as an artist at the Slade before entering the community, and her Stations of the Cross, carved in teak, and other works, are at the convent at Wantage.

Dog-tiredness is such a lovely prayer, really, if only we would recognize it as such. Sometimes I hear, 'I'm so dog-tired when I get to chapel, I can't pray'. But what does it matter? We don't matter. Our Lord can pray just as well through a dog-tired body and mind as through a well-rested one, better perhaps. It is the same with pain and suffering of all kinds. Our advance guard on the Infirmary Wing would tell us that.

(*Mother Maribel of Wantage*)

Likewise the Spirit helps us in our weakness; for we do not know how to pray as we ought, but that very Spirit intercedes with sighs too deep for words. (Romans 8.26)

> Drained of everything;
> hear my prayer, O God,
> and let my sigh come unto you.

SLEEP IS THE MYSTERY OF LIFE. (Henri Frederic Amiel)

THOMAS MERTON · *The world of business*

Thomas Merton (1915–68) was a North American Cistercian monk, author of many books, who lived his later years as a hermit and became increasingly interested in Eastern spirituality. He was accidentally electrocuted while attending an inter-faith conference in Bangkok. His published work reveals his own movement from a somewhat conservative and inward-looking piety to the passionate concern for justice of a 'guilty bystander'.

Businesses are, in reality, quasi-religious sects. When you go to work in one you embrace a *new faith*. And if they are really big businesses, you progress from faith to a kind of mystique. Belief in the product, preaching the product, in the end the product becomes the focus of a transcendental experience. Through 'the product' one communes with the vast forces of life, nature, and history that are expressed in business. Why not face it? Advertising treats all products with the reverence and the seriousness due to sacraments.

(Conjectures of a Guilty Bystander)

It is God's gift that all should eat and drink and take pleasure in all their toil. (Ecclesiastes 3.13)

> Give us, O God, the will and courage to struggle
> with what is complicated in our lives. Do not let us
> be content with easy solutions, but challenge us to
> live with integrity and pursue what is true.

WHAT GAIN HAVE THE WORKERS FROM THEIR TOIL? (Ecclesiastes 3.9)

EDWARD MIALL · *Good taste*

Edward Miall (1809–81), an independent minister, was a lifelong advocate of disestablishment of the Church of England. He was MP for Rochdale (1852–57) and Bradford (1869–74).

The etiquette of preaching prescribes an exclusively didactic style – and an address, the aim of which is to save souls, is supposed to approximate towards perfection, in proportion as it is free from conversational blemishes and inaccuracies, satisfies a fastidious and classical taste, and flows on in one unbroken stream from its commencement to its close. The consequence is, that while some few are pleased, and, perhaps, profited, the mass remain utterly untouched. Oh! for some revolution to break down for ever, and scatter to the four winds of heaven, our pulpit formulas and proprieties, and leave [people] at liberty to discourse on the sublime verities of the Christian faith, with the same freedom, variety, and naturalness, with which they would treat other subjects in other places!

(*The British Churches in Relation to the British People*)

The Teacher sought to find pleasing words, and he wrote words of truth plainly. (Ecclesiastes 12.10)

> Divine Word,
> may the words of those who speak in your name
> not set up road-blocks in the hearts and minds
> of those who seek you on their everyday paths.

AT THE NAME OF JESUS, EVERY VOICE GOES PLUMMY, EVERY GESTURE BECOMES PONTIFICAL, AND A FEARFUL CREEPING PARALYSIS SLOWS DOWN THE PACE OF THE DIALOGUE. (Dorothy L. Sayers)

JULES MONCHANIN · *Desert of temptation*

Jules Monchanin (1895–1957) was a French priest who spent the last eighteen years of his life in India, pursuing his ideal of a monastic life which should be 'totally Indian and totally Christian'.

Christ is thrust by the Spirit – who overshadowed his mother and whom he himself will send, another Paraclete – thrust into the desert. Forty days that recall the forty years. Exodus ends in this encounter between the Son of Jacob and the other angel: the Tempter. No manna: the calcined rocks he refused to change into bread. No miracles: weak like a man, he will not throw himself down from the roof of the Temple. No concupiscence for land or kingdoms. What was essential to the desert of exodus is all that remains in the desert of temptation: adoration and abandonment to God alone.

('The spirituality of the desert')

Therefore, as the Holy Spirit says,
'Today, if you hear his voice,
do not harden your hearts as in the rebellion,
    as on the day of testing in the wilderness,
where your ancestors put me to the test,
    though they had seen my works for forty years.'
(Hebrews 3.7–10, quoting from Psalm 95)

> No manna, no miracles, no greedy desires,
> but your life-giving love,
> the light of your countenance,
> unquenchably longed for!

THE DESERT AS A CITY OF SAINTS IS ONE THING; BUT WHAT ABOUT THE DESERT OF OUR CITIES? (Anonymous)

THOMAS MORE · *Fatherhood*

Thomas More (1478–1535), Roman Catholic, English humanist and friend of Erasmus, was Lord Chancellor in the reign of Henry VIII. On 6 July 1535 he was beheaded on Tower Hill for his treasonable refusal to acknowledge the king as head of the English Church.

Brutal and unworthy to be called father is he who does not himself weep at the tears of his child. How other fathers act I do not know, but you know well how gentle and devoted is my manner toward you, for I have always profoundly loved my own children and I have always been an indulgent parent – as every father ought to be. But at this moment my love has increased so much that it seems to me I used not to love you at all.

> (From a letter to his four children, probably written while he was away on a diplomatic mission in 1517)

'Do not be afraid, little flock, for it is your Father's good pleasure to give you the kingdom.' (Luke 12.32)

Abba!

THE VALUE OF MARRIAGE IS NOT THAT ADULTS PRODUCE CHILDREN BUT THAT CHILDREN PRODUCE ADULTS. (Peter De Vries)

WILLIAM MORRIS · *Art and the everyday*

William Morris (1834–96) was an artist, craftsman and writer, whose life aim became the integration of art and everyday life.

The chief source of art is man's pleasure in his daily necessary work, which expresses itself and is embodied in that work itself; nothing else can make the common surroundings of life beautiful, and whenever they are beautiful it is a sign that men's work has pleasure in it, however they may suffer otherwise.

(*Commonweal*)

Those who go out weeping,
  bearing the seed for sowing,
shall come home with shouts of joy,
  carrying their sheaves.
(Psalm 126.6)

> God of beauty, maker and mender,
> there is art that lights up the beloved everyday,
> and art that strikes our world like lightning,
> art that springs from joy
> and art that is sipped reluctantly from the cup of
>   despair:
>
> for all sparks from your divine fire
> be admiration, thanks and praise.

WHO FIRST INVENTED WORK – AND TIED THE FREE
AND HOLY-DAY REJOICING SPIRIT DOWN
TO THE EVER-HAUNTING IMPORTUNITY
OF BUSINESS? (Charles Lamb)

EDWIN MUIR · *Rediscovery*

Edwin Muir (1887–1959) was an Orkney-born poet and translator.

Last night, going to bed alone, I suddenly found myself (I was taking off my waistcoat) reciting the Lord's Prayer in a loud, emphatic voice – a thing I had not done for many years – with deep urgency and profound, disturbed emotion. While I went on I grew more composed; as if it had been empty and craving and were being replenished, my soul grew still; every word had a strange fullness of meaning which astonished and delighted me. It was late; I had sat up reading; I was sleepy; but as I stood in the middle of the floor half-undressed, saying the prayer over and over, meaning after meaning sprang from it, overcoming me again with joyful surprise; and I realized that this simple petition was always universal and always inexhaustible, and day by day sanctified human life.

(An Autobiography)

Then Jacob woke from his sleep and said, 'Surely the Lord is in this place – and I did not know it!' And he was afraid, and said, 'How awesome is this place! This is none other than the house of God, and this is the gate of heaven.' (Genesis 28.16–17)

> Our Father in heaven,
>   hallowed be your name.
> Your kingdom come.
> Your will be done,
>   on earth as it is in heaven.
> Give us this day our daily bread.
> And forgive us our debts,
>   as we also have forgiven our debtors.
> And do not bring us to the time of trial,
>   but rescue us from the evil one.
> For the kingdom, and the power, and the glory
>   are yours forever.
> (Matthew 6.9–13)

THE SOUND OF SURPRISE. (Whitney Balliett)

FLORENCE NIGHTINGALE ·
The Church and women

Florence Nightingale (1820–1910) became a nurse and devoted many years (in spite of her own indifferent health) to improving standards of nursing and public health.

The Church of England has for men bishoprics, archbishoprics, and a little work ... For women she has – what? I had no taste for theological discoveries. I would have given her my head, my hand, my heart. She would not have them. She did not know what to do with them. She told me to go back and do crochet in my mother's drawing-room; or, if I were tired of that, to marry and look well at the head of my husband's table. You may go to the Sunday School if you like, she said. But she gave me no training even for that. She gave me neither work to do for her, nor education for it.

> (To a clergyman who had asked her to use her influence to persuade his sister to remain in the Church of England)

Now there are varieties of gifts, but the same Spirit; and there are varieties of services, but the same Lord; and there are varieties of activities, but it is the same God who activates all of them in everyone. To each is given the manifestation of the Spirit for the common good. (1 Corinthians 12.4–7)

> For varieties of gifts, thanks to you.
> For opportunities for service, praise to you.
> For new vision, glory to you, our God.
> In your light may we see light
> and be light in the world's dark places.

SOME CALL IT OBSTINACY, OTHERS PERSEVERANCE. (Anonymous)

HENRI NOUWEN · *Eucharist*

Henri Nouwen (1932–1996) was a priest and popular author who spent the last years of his life living at L'Arche Daybreak community in Canada.

The Eucharist, sometimes, is celebrated with great ceremony, in splendid cathedrals and basilicas. But more often it is a 'small' event that few people know about. It happens in a living room, a prison cell, an attic – out of sight of the big movements of the world. It happens in secret, without vestments, candles, or incense. It happens with gestures so simple that outsiders don't even know that it takes place. But big or small, festive or hidden, it is the same event, revealing that life is stronger than death and love stronger than fear.

(With Burning Hearts)

When [Jesus] was at the table with them, he took bread, blessed and broke it, and gave it to them. Then their eyes were opened, and they recognized him. (Luke 24.30–31)

> Whether great ceremony or hidden meal,
> stir us, O God, to make
> eucharist that is bold and true.

FELLOWSHIP IS HEAVEN, AND LACK OF FELLOWSHIP IS HELL. (William Morris)

JOHN OMAN · *True faith*

John Oman (1860–1939) was a Presbyterian theologian.

The test of a true faith is the extent to which its religion is secular, the extent to which its special religious experiences are tested by the experiences of every day. In the life of Jesus nothing is more conspicuous than his meagre interest in specially sacred things, and his profound interest in the most ordinary things of the secular life. In his parables the only figures from the special religious life of a specially religious time are the Pharisee praying with himself in the temple, and the priest and the Levite turning aside on the road to Jericho – self-approving and little approved men, solitary to their heart's core. But what a varied secular procession of kings and slaves, and bailiffs and debtors, and farmers and fisher-folk, and housewives and children, and all at their secular occupations, with more feasting than fasting, and more marriages than funerals!

(Grace and Personality)

'Ought not this woman, a daughter of Abraham whom Satan bound for eighteen long years, be set free from this bondage on the sabbath day?' When [Jesus] said this, all his opponents were put to shame; and the entire crowd was rejoicing at all the wonderful things that he was doing. (Luke 13.16–17)

> May the world so loved by you, our God,
> rejoice in your good purposes,
> and co-operate in all your works.

EVERYTHING SHOUTED TO HIM OF THE GLORY OF GOD.
(E. Gilson, writing about Francis of Assisi)

SAMUEL PALMER ·
The difficult approach to creativity

Samuel Palmer (1805–81) was an English landscape painter and etcher, famous not least for the paintings produced between 1826 and 1835 when he was living in Shoreham, Kent, with a group of friends who called themselves 'The Ancients'. As a young man he was much influenced by his meeting and hearing William Blake.

I feel, ten minutes a day, the most ardent love for art, and spend the rest of my time in stupid apathy, negligence, ignorance, and restless despondency; without any of those delicious visions which are the only joys of my life – such as Christ at Emmaus; the repenting thief on the cross; the promise to Abraham; and secondary visions of the ages of chivalry, which are toned down with deep gold to distinguish them from the flashy, distracted present.

(From his notebooks)

To you, O Lord, I call;
   my rock, do not refuse to hear me,
for if you are silent to me,
   I shall be like those who go down to the Pit.
Hear the voice of my supplication,
   as I cry to you for help,
as I lift up my hands
   towards your most holy sanctuary.
(Psalm 28.1–2)

In times of cold and darkness
may we wait, and endure, and
keep our tools ready
to act once more when
your divine energy
returns.

QUESTIONER: SO YOU SPEND HALF AN HOUR A DAY IN PRAYER?
BISHOP MICHAEL RAMSEY: MAYBE TWO MINUTES IN PRAYER, BUT HALF AN HOUR WAITING AND PREPARING FOR IT. (Attributed)

SISTER PENELOPE · *Rainbow-redemption*

Sister Penelope CSMV, who wrote many books as 'A Religious of CSMV', was a member of the Anglican Community of St Mary the Virgin, Wantage.

We have some sort of illustration of this quite literally universal scope of the Redemption in the rainbow, that token of God's Covenant with Noah which to all time remains the symbol of His faithfulness. Made by the sunlight that has come through heaven to earth, it arches over earth as its immediate sphere; but, like all light that earth or any heavenly body either receives or gives, this light also streams outward into space. Further, in passing through earth's watery atmosphere – and mark the element – the single perfect light is broken up into its several parts. Of these the human eye sees seven colours only; but the unseen ultra-violet and infra-red light-rays act secretly and ceaselessly upon all life. So, since the Sun of Righteousness arose with healing in His wings, His varied light has been at work upon His whole creation. And even in its operation on mankind on earth there is always immeasurably more to it than we can ever see.

(As in Adam: A Study in the Church)

These are indeed but the outskirts of his ways;
  and how small a whisper do we hear of him!
(Job 26.14)

> Dear God,
> we who love the sun only less
> than the Sun of righteousness
> are hard-pressed sometimes
> in pursuit of your trackless goodness:
> keep us on the wide curve
> and narrow path of
> your rainbow promises.

THE CARCINOGENIC EFFECT OF OVER-DOSAGE [OF ULTRA-VIOLET RAYS] IS NOW RECOGNIZED. (*Chambers Science and Technology Dictionary*)

MARY PENINGTON · *True worship*

Mary Penington (c.1625–82), with her husband Isaac, found peace in worship with the Society of Friends (Quakers).

Thus, by taking up the cross, I received strength against many things which I had thought impossible to deny; but many tears did I shed, and bitterness of soul did I experience, before I came thither; and often cried out: 'I shall one day fall by the overpowering of the enemy.' But oh! the joy that filled my soul in the first meeting ever held in our house at Chalfont. To this day I have a fresh remembrance of it. It was then the Lord enabled me to worship Him in that which was undoubtedly his own, and fire up my whole strength, yea, to swim in the life which overcame me that day. Oh! long had I desired to worship Him with acceptation, and lift up my hands without doubting, which I witnessed that day in that assembly.

(*Experiences in the Life of Mary Penington, written by herself*)

Your words were found, and I ate them,
  and your words became to me a joy
  and the delight of my heart;
for I am called by your name,
  O Lord, God of hosts.
(Jeremiah 15.16)

     Protect me, O God, for in you I take refuge.
     You are my God; I have no good apart from you.
     Therefore my heart is glad, and my soul rejoices;
       and my body also rests secure.
     You show me the path of life.
     In your presence there is fullness of joy;
     In your right hand are pleasures forevermore.
     (adapted from Psalm 16)

THE BEST SURPRISES COME AS GIFTS AND NOT BECAUSE WE HAVE DESERVED THEM. (Anonymous)

KARL RAHNER · *The silence of the dead in God*

Karl Rahner (1904–84) was a Jesuit theologian, one of the most distinguished, influential and widely read of the generation of the Second Vatican Council.

Your Love has hidden itself in silence, so that my love can reveal itself in faith. You have left me, so that I can discover You ... Your silence in this time of my pilgrimage is nothing but the earthly manifestation of the eternal word of Your Love. That is how my dead imitate Your silence: they remain hidden from me because they have entered into Your Life ... Their silence is their loudest call to me, because it is the echo of Your silence. Their voice speaks in unison with Yours, trying to make itself heard above the noisy tumult of our incessant activity, competing with the anxious protestations of mutual love with which we poor humans try to reassure each other. Against all this, their voice and Yours strive to enwrap us and all our words in Your eternal silence.

(Encounters with Silence)

'If I go forward, he is not there;
    or backward, I cannot perceive him;
on the left he hides, and I cannot behold him;
    I turn to the right, but I cannot see him.'
(Job 23.8–9)

> O dazzling darkness
>   of the silent Word!
> Here is communion on earth
>   with the company of heaven.
> I will not let you go
>   until you bless me.

AND AFTER THE FIRE, A SOUND OF SHEER SILENCE. (1 Kings 19.12)

ARTHUR MICHAEL RAMSEY ·
Thinking it out

Arthur Michael Ramsey (1904–88) was the one hundredth Archbishop of Canterbury (1961–74). He was an eminent scholar who published many theological works. His strong commitment to church unity led him into dialogue with both the Pope and the Methodist Church.

Jesus appeals to the mind. Again and again he challenges his hearers to think. He doesn't reveal the truth to them in a kind of tabloid packet to be swallowed whole – 'Shut your eyes and swallow'. No, Jesus challenges his hearers, sowing seeds of truth in their minds and consciences, and then urging them to think out the meaning in it.

Think it out, think it out. It is in this process of thinking it out – together with the love and the will and the imagination – that Jesus and his message are made known.

(Through the Year with Michael Ramsey)

Let the same mind be in you that was in Christ Jesus.
(Philippians 2.5)

> Revealing God,
> open our eyes,
> unstop our ears,
> free our minds,
> enliven our hearts,
> that we may understand
> will all our being. ·

SECOND THOUGHTS ARE BEST. (Euripides)

RAINER MARIA RILKE · *True intimacy*

Rainer Maria Rilke (1875–1926) was an Austrian lyric poet, born in Prague. In earlier life he was influenced by Tolstoy and Russian pietism; later he abandoned mysticism for the aesthetic ideal.

But granted the consciousness that even between the closest friends there persist infinite distances, a wonderful living side by side can arise for them, if they succeed in loving the expanse between them which gives them the possibility of seeing one another in whole shape and before a great sky.

(*Letters to a Young Poet*)

Then he said, 'Jesus, remember me when you come into your kingdom.' He replied, 'Truly I tell you, today you will be with me in Paradise.' (Luke 23.42–3)

> I greet you.
> I give you space.
> We move on,
> huge in our togetherness.

It is a mistake to suppose that God is only, or even chiefly, concerned with religion. (William Temple)

77

JOHN A. T. ROBINSON · *New images*

John A. T. Robinson (1919–83) was the Anglican Bishop of Woolwich when he published his famous book Honest to God, *which became a best-seller and scandalized Christian conservatives.*

What looks like being required of us, reluctant as we may be for the effort involved, is a radically new mould, or *meta-morphosis*, of Christian belief and practice. Such a recasting will, I am convinced, leave the fundamental truth of the Gospel unaffected. But it means that we have to be prepared for *everything* to go into the melting – even our most cherished religious categories and moral absolutes. And the first thing we must be ready to let go is our image of God himself.

(*Honest to God*)

She is easily discerned by those who love her,
and is found by those who seek her.
She hastens to make herself known to those who
    desire her.
(Wisdom 6.12–13)

> God our Mother, sustain us;
> God our Sister, redeem us;
> God all-vulnerable, sanctify us.

NOSTALGIA ISN'T WHAT IT USED TO BE. (Anonymous)

OSCAR ROMERO · *Truth*

Oscar Romero (1917–80) was for three years the Roman Catholic Archbishop of San Salvador, in the Central American republic of El Salvador. He dedicated his life to the service of the poor and oppressed, and on 24 March 1980 he was assassinated as he preached in his own cathedral.

If there is not truth in love, there is hypocrisy.

Often, fine words are said, handshakes given, perhaps even a kiss, but at bottom there is no truth.

A civilization where the trust of one for another is lost, where there is so much lying and no truth, has no foundation of love. There can't be love where there is falsehood.

Our environment lacks truth. And when the truth is spoken, it gives offence, and the voices that speak the truth are put to silence.

(From a homily)

You will know the truth and the truth will make you free.
(John 8.32)

From the falsehood of despair, good Lord deliver us.

PILATE ASKED HIM, 'WHAT IS TRUTH?' (John 18.38)

MARK RUTHERFORD · *Looking*

Mark Rutherford was the pseudonym of William Hale White (1831–1913). He qualified for the Congregational ministry, but was expelled for his views on inspiration. He became a civil servant, journalist and writer, best known for a series of novels.

Early morning before sunrise: the valley was filled with mist; red clouds in the sky. For a minute or two the mist took the colour, but fainter, of the clouds. What patience is required in order to see! The sun had not risen, the grass in the field was obviously green, but not without intent fixture of the eyes upon it was the dark twilight shade of green recognised which was its peculiar meaning and beauty. To most of us, perhaps not to artists, it is more difficult to look than to think.

(More Pages from a Journal)

[Elisha] replied, 'Do not be afraid, for there are more with us than there are with them.' Then Elisha prayed: 'O Lord, please open his eyes that he may see.' So the Lord opened the eyes of the servant, and he saw; the mountain was full of horses and chariots of fire all around Elisha. (2 Kings 6.16–17)

> O God,
> let us behold your glory –
> but not too much of it.

WHAT YOU ARE YOU DO NOT SEE, WHAT YOU SEE IS YOUR SHADOW. (Rabindranath Tagore)

MAY SARTON · *The cat*

May Sarton (1912–95) was born in Europe and lived most of her life on the east coast of America. An internationally acclaimed poet and novelist, she is also well known and much loved for her autobiographical works.

When I talk about solitude I am really talking also about making space for that intense, hungry face at the window, starved cat, starved person. It is making space to *be there*. Lately a small tabby cat has come every day and stared at me with a strange, intense look. Of course I put food out, night and morning. She is so terrified that she runs away at once when I open the door, but she comes back to eat ravenously as soon as I disappear. Yet her hunger is clearly not only for food. I long to take her in my arms and hear her purr with relief at finding shelter. Will she ever become tame enough for that, to give in to what she longs to have? It is such an intense look with which she scans my face at the door before she runs away. It is not a pleading look, simply a huge question: 'Can I trust?' Our two gazes hang on its taut thread. I find it painful.

(Journal of a Solitude)

Welcome one another, therefore, just as Christ has welcomed you, for the glory of God. (Romans 15.7)

> Loving God,
> show us the gift and cost of connection.
> May we love and redeem one another
> even as you love and redeem us.

Jesus looked at him. (Luke 18.24)

DOROTHY L. SAYERS · *Image and reality*

Dorothy L. Sayers (1893–1957), perhaps best known for her detective fiction, was also a dramatist, theologian and translator of Dante. In her later writing she was much influenced (as here) by the ideas of Charles Williams (see p. 98).

The great thing, I am sure, is not to be nervous about God – not to try to shut out the Lord Immanuel from *any* sphere of truth. Art is not He – we must not substitute Art for God; yet this also is He, for it is one of His Images and therefore reveals His nature. Here we see in a mirror darkly – we behold only the images; elsewhere we shall see face to face, in the place where Image and Reality are one.

('Towards a Christian aesthetic')

In his own image God made humankind. (Genesis 9.6)

They have cast an image for themselves. (Deuteronomy 9.12)

> God, who fearfully and wonderfully
> made us strange and marvellous co-makers:
> may all our makings, in sight and sound,
>   in solid matter,
>   in the mind's dreaming,
>   and in ourselves,
> open our eyes to ever-new vistas of
>   your infinite goodness.

AN ARTIST IS A DREAMER CONSENTING TO DREAM OF THE ACTUAL WORLD. (George Santayana)

VIDA SCUDDER · *Spiritual landscapes*

Vida Scudder (1861–1954), a North American literary scholar, Christian socialist and social activist, also belonged to a group of women dedicated to prayer and intercession for social justice.

Reality ... is in relationship alone. This is true, not only on the natural plane, where consciousness, forever baffled, yet persists in contemplating one or another spiritual landscape, and in endeavouring to report and verify what is revealed. I know God only as I know the view; and your view can not be mine. Yet the vision vouchsafed to you and me by 'sight of soul', to use the beautiful medieval phrase, is authentic, and summoning. That it is ultimate reality, no one dares assume. But it has reality for me. And the landscape beckons. *Laus Deo* [Praise God]!

(*On Journey*)

By faith Moses ... persevered, as though he saw him who is invisible. (Hebrews 11.27)

> Faith and sight are set against each other,
> but surely this is a mistake:
> faith sees and seeing believes –
> believes what it sees, and
> by faith sees you,
> in whose invisible light we truly see.

THE CAPACITY FOR SEEING IS DEPENDENT ON THE INCAPACITY OF THE EYE TO SEE ITSELF. (Viktor Frankl)

HANNAH WHITALL SMITH · *Old age*

Hannah Whitall Smith (1832–1911) was a Quaker and a founder member of the Women's Christian Movement and of the suffrage movement in the USA.

I am convinced it is a great art to know how to grow old gracefully, and I am determined to practise it ... I always thought I should love to grow old, and I find it even more delightful than I thought. It is so delicious to be *done* with things, and to feel no need any longer to concern myself much about earthly affairs ... I am tremendously content to let one activity after another go, and to wait quietly and happily the opening of the door at the end of the passage-way, that will let me in to my real abiding place.

(From a letter)

Listen to me, O house of Jacob,
   all the remnant of the house of Israel,
who have been borne by me from your birth,
   carried from the womb;
even to your old age I am he,
   even when you turn grey I will carry you.
I have made, and I will bear;
   I will carry and will save.
(Isaiah 46.3–4)

Dear God,
I used to think I'd love growing old –
'It gets better every year', I used to say –
but standing unsteadily on the downward slope,
I know I don't want to give up anything
yet – yet I want to be ready
when the time comes
to pass through that gateway,
neither resigned nor defiant
but expectant.

IT NEVER SEEMS THE RIGHT MOMENT TO DIE. (R. M. Benson)

ADRIENNE VON SPEYR · *Essential dialogue*

Adrienne von Speyr (1902–67), was the mystic with whom the Swiss Catholic theologian Hans Urs von Balthasar formed a secular institute after he had left the Jesuits. Her religious experiences provided him with inspiration for his theological work.

Much that people who love one another do not express is essentially word nevertheless. And every word spoken in God, whether it is the word of God or a human word, is really and essentially spoken, though it need not be articulate. God and human beings do not remain imprisoned within themselves in silence; it is not as though conversation were superfluous because everything were known. The dialogue is so essential and profound that simply being together fulfils the role of speech. It becomes superfluous for the word to be conscious, articulate and felt. Mutual contemplation is a dialogue.

(*The Word*)

Thus the Lord used to speak to Moses face to face as one speaks to a friend. (Exodus 33.11)

> You and I
> (my God –)
> I and you
> (– and all things!)

'WHEN *I* USE A WORD ... IT MEANS JUST WHAT I CHOOSE IT TO MEAN – NEITHER MORE NOR LESS.'
(Humpty Dumpty, in *Through the Looking-Glass* by Lewis Carroll)

ELIZABETH CADY STANTON · *Revolution*

Elizabeth Cady Stanton (1815–1902) was a North American social reformer and women's suffrage leader. When she married in 1840 she insisted on leaving out the word 'obey' from the marriage vows.

Others say it is not *politic* to rouse religious opposition. This much-lauded policy is but another word for *cowardice*. How can woman's position be changed from that of a subordinate to an equal, without opposition, without the broadest discussion of all the questions involved in her present degradation? For so far-reaching and momentous a reform as her complete independence, an entire revolution in all existing institutions is inevitable.

(Introduction to *The Woman's Bible*)

'Do not think that I have come to bring peace to the earth; I have not come to bring peace, but a sword.' (Matthew 10.34)

> Transforming God,
> give us big hearts and good friends
> as we seek to change the world.

IF OUR REVOLUTION DOES NOT HAVE THE GOAL OF CHANGING MEN, IT DOESN'T INTEREST ME. (Che Guevara)

CAROLINE STEPHEN · *Simplicity*

Caroline Stephen (1834–1909) was a British Quaker and author of the Quaker classic, Quaker Strongholds, *published in 1890.*

It is, indeed, not easy to define the precise kind or amount of luxury which is incompatible with Christian simplicity; or rather it must of necessity vary. But the principle is, I think, clear. In life, as in art, whatever does not help, hinders. All that is superfluous to the main object of life must be cleared away, if that object is to be fully attained. In all kinds of effort, whether moral, intellectual, or physical, the essential condition of vigour is a severe pruning away of redundance. Is it likely that the highest life, the life of the Christian body, can be carried on upon easier terms?

(*Quaker Strongholds*)

'For where your treasure is, there your heart will be also.'
(Luke 12.34)

> God of life,
> help us know where our treasure lies,
> and give us that freedom of spirit
> whereby we do not need to cling
> either to possessions or to one another.

THE SUPERFLUOUS, A VERY NECESSARY THING. (Voltaire)

CHARLES LOTHIAN SUMNER ·
Relationships in heaven

Charles Lothian Sumner (1901–70) – Brother Lothian – was a member of the Anglican Society of St Francis.

Somebody died. 'What a loss!' 'The work will suffer!' We look solemn when we talk about the dead, especially when we don't know them very well. But inside – was there a sense of relief, of ashamed thankfulness? Never to have to feel small, insecure, second-rate again ...? Higher and higher praise covers up this 'we shall never meet again – thank God'.

But is this really true? Does death really end a relationship? What about all the other relationships? We thank God for continuing life and relationships – the *right* ones. Have we not to reject *all* relationships after death, or expect to take them up again – *all* of them? Are there no unpleasant moments in heaven? Does death really land us in heaven brimming over with love for the people we don't like very much? God does not seem to work flashing changes in us. Perhaps this is where purgatory comes in: forgiveness is to be worked out in the end. Maybe God can't get rid of us any more than we can get rid of him. We don't know who our neighbours will be in heaven.

(Notes taken from a sermon)

And the leaves of the tree are for the healing of the nations. (Revelation 22.2)

> At your right hand, O God,
> is pleasure for evermore:
> fit us in this life for your presence
> and for the company you keep.

JERUSALEM THE GOLDEN ...
I KNOW NOT, O I KNOW NOT WHAT SOCIAL JOYS ARE THERE!
(Bernard of Cluny, trans. J. M. Neale)

PIERRE TEILHARD DE CHARDIN ·
Transformation

Pierre Teilhard de Chardin (1881–1955) was a French Jesuit theologian,
palaeontologist and philosopher. His researches increasingly took him away
from Jesuit orthodoxy and he was forbidden by his superiors to publish or teach.
His best-known works, The Phenomenon of Man *and* Le Milieu Divin, *were*
published after his death.

It is a terrifying thing to have been born: I mean, to find oneself,
without having willed it, swept irrevocably along on a torrent of
fearful energy which seems as though it wished to destroy
everything it carries with it.

What I want, my God, is that by a reversal of forces which you
alone can bring about, my terror in face of the nameless changes
destined to renew my being may be turned into an overflowing joy
at being transformed into you.

(Hymn of the Universe)

'The wind blows where it chooses, and you hear the sound of it,
but you do not know where it comes from or where it goes. So it
is with everyone who is born of the Spirit.' (John 3.8)

> Dear God, hold us when we are afraid;
> stand with us when we cannot stand alone.
> Protect us from evil,
> deliver us from paralysis, and
> lead us gently into the future.

GOD IS ETERNALLY PREGNANT. (Meister Eckhart)

SYBIL THORNDIKE · *Wartime*

Sybil Thorndike (1882–1976) was one of the greatest actresses of her day, often collaborating with her husband, Sir Lewis Casson.

2 June 1940

Darling John,
We were so thrilled to get your letter yesterday morning, and we won't worry. We'll just hold on to the splendid thought of all being well with you ... I find churchmen's talk quite irritating ... Ann brought me a pamphlet yesterday about fortitude and suffering and death being sacramental, etc. Honestly, I think that begs the whole question. If Christianity is this superstitious thing, then the sooner it's overboard the better. I find the thing I'm striving towards is at once much simpler and much more profound – and *in* everything, as you say – the god of the 'something – calculus' in mathematics, the utter rightness and beauty of a complicated bit of counterpoint – well – well!

(Letter to her son, John Casson)

How weighty to me are your thoughts, O God!
　　How vast is the sum of them!
I try to count them – they are more than the sand;
　　I come to the end – I am still with you.
(Psalm 139.17–18)

　　　　God,
　　　　I love you –
　　　　because you are utterly simple
　　　　and because you simply ARE.

... PROMPT ME, GOD;
BUT NOT YET. (R. S. Thomas)

PAUL TILLICH · *God*

Paul Tillich (1886–1965) was a German-born American Protestant theologian and philosopher. An early critic of Hitler, he explains religion as a matter of 'ultimate concern'. His major work was his three-volume Systematic Theology.

The name of this infinite and inexhaustible depth and ground of all being is *God*. That depth is what the word *God* means. And if that word has not much meaning for you, translate it, and speak of the depths of your life, of the source of your being, of your ultimate concern, of what you take seriously without any reservation.

(*The Shaking of the Foundations*)

O the depth of the riches and wisdom and knowledge of God! How unsearchable are his judgements and how inscrutable his ways! (Romans 11.33)

> Where can I escape from your spirit,
> where flee from your presence?
> You know me through and through;
> there is nothing hidden from you.
> Whatever I call you – it's the same.
> (based on Psalm 139)

WITH A NAME LIKE YOURS, YOU MIGHT BE ANY SHAPE.
(Lewis Carroll, *Through the Looking-Glass*)

PHILIP TOYNBEE · *Mutuality*

Philip Toynbee (1916–81) was a poet, novelist, reviewer and, in the last five years of his life, diarist. His diary displays his increasing interest in the 'holy mysteries that surround us all'.

The Incarnation. Believing that God could be seen with *extraordinary* clarity in Jesus, we recognise all the better that God can be seen with *ordinary but perpetually surprising* clarity in our wife, our friend, our ward-mate in hospital ...

The little woman in her sixties coming into my room to tell me about her friend who had just been brought in with what must have seemed like a serious cancer. She started talking about prayer, and we found that we agreed exactly about what it should and shouldn't be. 'Thanks for the help you've given me,' she said as she left, and I thanked her back, and both of us were speaking the truth.

(End of a Journey)

'Whoever welcomes the one I send, welcomes me, and whoever welcomes me, welcomes the one who sent me.' (John 13.20, New Jerusalem Bible)

> God,
> we look for you in holy places
> but you are outside the gates;
> we greet our friend
> and your love greets us
>   from our friend's lips and eyes and hand.
> Worrying over problems, we are restless and
>   ignorant;
> conferring with a friend,
> we find both wisdom and insight.
> For this, we love and honour you
> – all for yourself.

DYING HAS NOT BEEN MUCH WRITTEN ABOUT BY THOSE WHO ARE EXPERIENCING IT. (Philip Toynbee)

GEORGE TYRRELL · *Return of the prodigal*

George Tyrrell (1861–1909) was an Irish theologian, a convert to Roman Catholicism; he became a Jesuit, but was eventually expelled from the Society for his Modernist views.

After the history of my decadence and depravity it would be pleasant to tell of some blinding light, some clear call from death unto life; but miracles are not common, and I seemed to wander back to the better way as casually and crookedly as I had wandered away from it. Indeed the spoiling and tangling of one's soul is easy and rapid compared with the tedious labour of disentanglement ... I drifted into the Church for a thousand paltry motives and reasons; some good, some bad; some true, some false or fallacious – much as an ignorant and drunken navigator gets his vessel into the right port by a mere fluke. I am more satisfied to think, as I fondly perhaps do, that my lots were in other hands – at least I still hope so.

(From his autobiography)

'When [the younger son] came to himself he said, "How many of my father's hired hands have bread enough and to spare, but here I am dying of hunger! I will get up and go to my father, and I will say to him, 'Father, I have sinned against heaven and before you; I am no longer worthy to be called your son; treat me like one of your hired hands.'"' (Luke 15.17–19)

> God,
> you outride justice
> and severity of judgement,
> and those who,
> wayward and rebellious,
> drift back to you,
> are welcomed by your
> merciful laughter.

PEOPLE WROTE WELCOMES TO HIM ON THEIR DOORS.
(said of Crates the Cynic)

EVELYN UNDERHILL · *Action and adoration*

Evelyn Underhill (1875–1941) was one of Anglicanism's most distinguished writers on mysticism, and a pioneer among spiritual directors in the twentieth century.

Adoration can never exempt the Christian from this-world action; and this-world action, however beneficial, will fail of effect if its foundations are not based upon the life of adoration. To go back to Brother Giles's parable, the sparrow must go to the mountain; but it must also live the common sparrow life, build its nest, and feed its young. The awed sense of the mystery in which we live, and which enfolds and penetrates us, must not stultify our small human activities, but improve them. It is by this alternation of the transcendent and the homely, the interaction of lofty thought and concrete living – all the fiction and effort consequent on our two-levelled human life – that true growth of human personality is achieved.

('The Christian basis of social action')

Even the sparrow finds a home,
   and the swallow a nest for herself,
   where she may lay her young,
at your altars, O Lord of hosts,
   my King and my God ...
No good thing does the Lord withhold
   from those who walk uprightly.
O Lord of hosts,
   happy is everyone who trusts in you.
(Psalm 84.3, 11–12)

      Go-between God,
      inweave the fabric of our common life,
      that the many-coloured beauty of your love
      may find expression in all our exchanges.

WITHOUT WORSHIP YOU SHRINK; IT'S AS BRUTAL AS THAT.
(Peter Shaffer, *Equus*)

MAX WARREN · *The unnoticed*

Max Warren (1904–77) was general secretary of the Church Missionary Society.

[The fourth category of the laity] is the great majority of the People of God, whose life and witness will lie in their integrity, in their devotion to duty in the hum-drum of life. These are not called to struggle in 'the high places of the field': they are not chosen to exercise a prophetic role of challenge in the place where they work: these are the *unnoticed* who carry the world on the shoulders of their fidelity. Without the flavour of their saltiness the fabric of human society would decay or fail of redemption. They are the home-makers, wives and mothers who make Christian hospitality possible: they are the small shopkeepers who scorn to give short measure: they are the bus conductors whose patience and good humour under much tribulation sweeten our journeyings: they are the men and women who provide our food, planting and reaping, processing and purveying, the great company of those who never see the issue of their toil, but who endure as seeing Him who is invisible: these are they who make a neighbourhood good because they are good neighbours.

(Perspective in Mission)

As [Jesus] was getting into the boat, the man who had been possessed by demons begged him that he might be with him. But Jesus refused, and said to him, 'Go home to your friends, and tell them how much the Lord has done for you, and what mercy he has shown you.' (Mark 5.18–19)

> God of Jesus,
> reveal to us the value and meaning
> of the little things in life.
> Bless our homes and the homes of our friends,
> that they may be places of happy meeting.

WE ARE ALL SPECIAL CASES. (Albert Camus)

ALAN WATTS · *Holy humour*

Alan Watts (1915-73) was one of the most significant and charismatic of the leaders of the 1960s' hippy movement in San Francisco. While still at school, he had become a Buddhist, and became an Anglican priest ten years later, before returning to his passion for Zen. A man of contradictions, he was treated by many as a guru, despite real wildness in his own personal life. He died when he was only 58.

Holiness is close to, but not quite the same as, a return to innocence and to the life of spontaneous impulse ... For holiness is the life of spontaneity and self-abandonment *with humour*, which includes the wisdom of serpents as well as the gentleness of doves, because humour is nothing other than perfect self-awareness. It is the delighted recognition of one's own absurdity, and a loving cynicism with regard to one's pretensions. A person who has learned to be *fully* self-aware can safely return to living by impulse. Humour is the transformation of anxiety into laughter: the same trembling, but with a different meaning. Holy humour is the discovery of the ultimate joke on oneself.

(*Beyond Theology*)

Abraham was a hundred years old when his son Isaac was born to him. Now Sarah said, 'God has brought laughter for me; everyone who hears will laugh with me.' (Genesis 21.5–6)

> Teach us, dear God,
> to see ourselves as you see us,
> and then to laugh.

FOR EVERYTHING THERE IS A SEASON: ...
A TIME TO WEEP, AND A TIME TO LAUGH. (Ecclesiastes 3.1, 4)

SIMONE WEIL · *Tolerance?*

Simone Weil (1909–43) was a French philosopher and religious writer, who combined 'the most sophisticated scholarly and philosophical interests with an extreme moral intensity and a dedicated identification with the interests of the oppressed and exploited' (Chambers Biographical Dictionary).

Religion has been proclaimed a private affair. According to present-day habits of mind, this doesn't mean that it resides in the secret places of the soul, in that inner sanctuary where even the individual conscience doesn't penetrate. It means that it is a matter of choice, opinion, taste, almost of caprice, something like the choice of a political party, or even that of a tie...

What is comical about the situation is that religion, that is to say, [the human being's] relation to God, is not nowadays regarded as too sacred a matter to be interfered with by any outside authority, but is placed among the things which the State leaves to each one's own particular fancy, as being of small importance from the point of view of public affairs. At least, that has been the case in the recent past, and that is the contemporary meaning attached to the word 'tolerance'.

(The Need for Roots)

'I will take you as my people, and I will be your God.'
(Exodus 6.7)

> Awaken all your peoples, O God,
> in times when the community of faith is divided,
> and belief in you brings no privileges
> except the heavy burden of faded glories
> and dwindling respect.
> Let us not fall asleep at our separate devotions,
> but seek your kingdom and your righteousness
> always and everywhere.

WE HAVE JUST ENOUGH RELIGION TO MAKE US HATE, BUT NOT ENOUGH TO MAKE US LOVE ONE ANOTHER. (Jonathan Swift)

CHARLES WILLIAMS · *Eros and Agape*

Charles Williams (1886–1945) was an English poet, theologian, critic, novelist, teacher of the 'way of the affirmation of images'.

Eros need not be for ever on his knees to Agape; he has a right to his delights; they are part of the Way. The division is not between the Eros of the flesh and the Agape of the soul; it is between the moment of love which sinks into hell and the moment which rises to the in-Godding. Beatrice will, no doubt, 'die'. But the eyes from which Love shot his earlier arrows, the eyes which ... have the power to clear [Dante's] blindness, the eyes which are in heaven so full of love for him, the eyes in which the two-natured Gryphon of Christ is reflected, the eyes of the Florentine girl – there are the eyes which in the end change only into the eyes of the Mother of God. This is the unique and lasting mystery of the Way.

(*Religion and Love in Dante*)

The mandrakes give forth fragrance,
   and over our doors are all choice fruits,
new as well as old,
   which I have laid up for you, O my beloved.
(Song of Solomon 7.13)

> Lord Jesus Christ, God with us,
> let it not be said of us
> that we think lightly of God's gifts;
> but let us live, embodied, in your love,
> as for love you lived, embodied, among us.

I HOLD THIS THE HIGHEST TASK FOR A BOND BETWEEN TWO PEOPLE: THAT EACH PROTECTS THE SOLITUDE OF THE OTHER. (R. M. Rilke)

JOHN WOOLMAN · *Outward business*

John Woolman (1720–72), American Quaker, gave up his business to give time to persuading everyone he could that buying and selling their fellow-human beings was not an appropriate activity for humans.

The increase of business became my burden, for though my natural inclination was toward merchandise, yet I believed Truth required me to live more free from outward cumbers and there was now a strife in my mind between the two; and in this exercise my prayers were put up to the Lord, who graciously heard me and gave me a heart resigned to his holy will. Then I lessened my outward business ... and so in a while wholly laid down merchandise, following my trade as a tailor, myself only, having no apprentice. I also had a nursery of apple trees, in which I employed some of my time – hoeing, grafting, trimming, and innoculating.

(Journal)

And Amaziah [the priest at Bethel] said to Amos, 'O seer, go, flee away to the land of Judah, earn your bread there, and prophesy there; but never again prophesy at Bethel, for it is the king's sanctuary, and it is a temple of the kingdom.'
    Then Amos answered Amaziah, 'I am no prophet, nor a prophet's son; but I am a herdsman, and a dresser of sycamore trees, and the Lord took me from following the flock, and the Lord said to me, "Go, prophesy to my people Israel".'
(Amos 7.12–15)

> God, when there are hard choices to be made
> may we listen and wait,
> act and follow,
> without haste and without rest,
> the way of your love.

It is an unhappy business that God has given to human beings to be busy with. (Ecclesiastes 1.13)

OLIVE WYON · *Grown-ups*

Olive Wyon (1881–1966), a gifted translator of German theological works, served with the London Missionary Society and was principal of the Church of Scotland's St Colm's Missionary College. Her contemplative spirituality shows her strong commitment to ecumenism and community.

The spiritual life means growth. We are called to grow 'unto the measure of the stature of the fullness of Christ'. The end of growth is perfection: this means both purity of heart and maturity of character. Just as the hyacinth in its pure beauty develops from a dark and uninteresting bulb, through all the stages of growth, into a perfect bloom, so this purity or perfection means reaching the end for which we have been made. Thus the mature Christian is not a blameless, insipid kind of person, out of touch with real life, but rather a wise, all-round, 'grown-up' kind of person; one who is always moving on, and finding more in life and in people and in God, to the very end.

(*On the Way*)

'If you wish to be perfect, go, sell your possessions, and give the money to the poor, and you will have treasure in heaven; then come, follow me.' (Matthew 19.21)

> God, give us
> the guts to live life to the full.
> Give us generous hearts,
> thirsty souls, and
> fiery spirits.
> Give us resurrection.
> Give us yourself.

THE YOUNG MAN ... WENT AWAY GRIEVING, FOR HE HAD MANY POSSESSIONS. (Matthew 19.22)

SOURCES AND ACKNOWLEDGEMENTS

These are listed according to the order of entries.

Aelred of Rievaulx, *On Spiritual Friendship* 3.96–7; compilers' paraphrase.

J. H. Oldham, *Florence Allshorn and the Story of St Julian's* (SCM Press, 1951). Used by permission.

Humphrey Carpenter, *W. H. Auden: A Biography* (George Allen & Unwin, 1981), quoting from a sermon in the possession of Janet Carleton.

Monica Baldwin, *I Leap over the Wall* (Hamish Hamilton, 1951).

Basil of Caesarea, Letters XII and XIII; compilers' translation.

Richard Baxter, *Reliquiae Baxterianae*, ed. Matthew Sylvester (1696).

The Narrative of the Persecution of Agnes Beaumont in 1674 (Constable & Co., undated).

Julia de Beausobre, *Creative Suffering* (SLG Press, 1984), copyright Estate of Julia de Beausobre. Used by permission.

Rule of St Benedict, chapter 31, compilers' translation.

Kathleen Bliss, *The Future of Religion* (C. A. Watts & Co., 1969).

Dietrich Bonhoeffer, *Letters and Papers from Prison* (SCM Press, 1971). Used by permission.

Elizabeth Bowen, *A Time in Rome* (Alfred A. Knopf, Inc., 1959). Used by permission.

Martin Buber, *I and Thou* , trans. Ronald Gregor Smith, second (revised) edition, T. & T. Clark, 1958). Used by permission.

Lewis Gibbs (ed.) *The Diary of Fanny Burney* (J. M. Dent, 1940).

E. Moberley Bell, *Josephine Butler: Flame of Fire* (Constable & Co., 1962).

Frank Houghton, *Amy Carmichael of Dohnavur: The Story of a Lover and Her Beloved* (SPCK, 1953).

Carlo Carretto, *In Search of the Beyond*, trans. S. Fawcett (copyright DLT and Orbis Books, 1975). Used by permission of the publishers.

V. M. Carver, *The Great Shift: Life Seen as Sacramental* (Community of St Clare, 1977). Used by permission of the Community of St Clare.

Irene Claremont de Castillejo, *Knowing Woman: A Feminine Psychology* (Harper & Row, 1974); Used by permission of Shambhala Publications, Inc., 300 Massachusetts Avenue, Boston, MA.

M. M. Philipon, *The Spiritual Doctrine of Sister Elizabeth of the Trinity*, trans. by a Benedictine of Stanbrook Abbey (Westminster MD: Newman Press, 1948).

R. J. Armstrong and I. C. Brady (eds and trans), *Francis and Clare: The Complete Works* (Paulist Press, 1982). Used by permission of the publishers.

Liz Stanley (ed.), *The Diaries of Hannah Cullwick* (Virago Press, 1983).

Elizabeth David, *English Bread and Yeast Cookery* (Penguin Books, 1977).

Joy Davidman, *Smoke on the Mountain: An Interpretation of the Ten Commandments in Terms of To-day* (Hodder & Stoughton, 1957). Copyright Estate of the late Joy Davidman. Used by permission.

Thomas H. Johnson and Theodora Ward (eds), *Letters of Emily Dickinson* (The Belknap Press of Harvard University Press, 1958).

C. H. Dodd, *The Interpretation of the Fourth Gospel* (Cambridge University Press, 1960). Used by permission.

Catherine de Hueck Doherty, *Welcome, Pilgrim* (Madonna House Publications, 1991). Used by permission of the publishers.

John Donne, *Complete Poetry and Selected Prose*, ed. John Hayward (Nonesuch Press, 1990).

R. E. Whitson (ed.), *The Shakers: Two Centuries of Spiritual Reflection* (Paulist Press, 1983). Used by permission of the publishers.

A. M. Farrer, *A Science of God?* (Geoffrey Bles, 1966). Copyright Estate of Katherine Farrer. Used by permission.

H. van Etten, *George Fox and the Quakers*, trans. E. Kelvin Osborne (New York and London: Harper Torchbooks and Longmans, Green & Co, undated).

Douglas V. Steere (ed.), *Quaker Spirituality* (Paulist Press, 1984), quoting from *Memoir of the Life of Elizabeth Fry ... edited by two of her daughters*. Used by permission of the publishers.

Ida Friederike Görres, *Broken Lights: Diaries and Letters 1951–1959*, trans. Barbara Waldstein-Wartenberg (Burns & Oates, 1964).

Caroline Graveson, *Religion and Culture*, Swarthmore Lecture, 1937 (George Allen & Unwin, 1937).

Gregory of Nyssa, *The Life of Moses*, source of translation unknown.

Mother Columba Hart OSB (trans.), *Hadewijch: The Complete Works* (Paulist Press, 1980). Used by permission of the publishers.

Peter Dronke, *Women Writers of the Middle Ages: A Critical Study of Texts from Perpetua to Marguerite Porete* (Cambridge University Press, 1984). Used by permission.

Etty Hillesum, *Etty: A Diary 1941–43* (Jonathan Cape, 1983). Used by permission of Random House UK and Uitgeverij Balans (Amsterdam).

Shirley Tunnicliff (ed.), *The Selected Letters of Mary Hobhouse* (Wellington, New Zealand: Daphne Brasell Associates Press, 1992). Used by permission.

Catherine Phillips (ed.), *Gerard Manley Hopkins* (Oxford University Press, 1986). Extract from letter used by permission of the publishers.

Gwendolen Green (ed.), *Letters from Baron Friedrich von Hügel to a Niece* (J. M. Dent, 1928).

Linda Brent [pseudonym of Harriet Ann Jacobs], *Incidents in the Life of a Slave Girl: Written by Herself* (Boston, 1861).

Richard Jefferies, *The Story of My Heart: My Autobiography* (Longman, Green and Co., 1883; Quartet Books Ltd, 1979).

Jerome, Letter 52.8 (compilers' translation).

Jerome K. Jerome, *Three Men in a Boat* (1889).

Pope John XXIII, *Journal of a Soul* (Geoffrey Chapman, 1965).

Sebastian Brock (trans.), *The Syriac Fathers on Prayer and the Spiritual Life* (Cistercian Publications, 1987).

Rufus M. Jones, *Finding the Trail of Life* (George Allen & Unwin, 1926).

Helen Joseph, *Side by Side* (Zed Books Ltd, 1986). Used by permission of the publishers.

Julian of Norwich, *A Revelation of Love*, compilers' translation.

Kathy Keay (ed.), *Laughter, Silence and Shouting: An Anthology of Women's Prayers* (HarperCollins, 1994). Used by permission.

Søren Kierkegaard, *Gospel of Sufferings*, trans A. S. Aldworth and W. S. Ferrie (James Clark & Co., 1955).

Francis Kilvert, *Kilvert's Diary*, three vols, ed. W. Plomer (Jonathan Cape Ltd, 1938-44). Copyright Estate of William Plomer. Used by permission.

Frank Lake, *Clinical Theology*, abridged by Martin H. Yeomans (Darton, Longman & Todd, 1986). Used by permission.

Charles Lamb, 'Grace before meat', *The Essays of Elia* (1823).

Lucy Larcom, *A New England Girlhood* (Boston and New York: Houghton, Mifflin Co., 1889).

C. S. Lewis, *A Grief Observed* (Faber & Faber, 1961). Used by permission of Faber & Faber (London) and of HarperCollins Publishers (New York).

Helen M. Luke, *Woman: Earth and Spirit, The Feminine in Symbol and Myth* (New York: Crossroad, 1987). Copyright 1981, Helen M. Luke. All rights reserved. Used with permission of the publishers.

Makereti (Maggie Papakura), *The Old-Time Maori* (Victor Gollancz, 1938). Used by permission of the publishers.

John Macmurray, *Reason and Emotion* (Faber & Faber, 1962). Used by permission.

Sister Thekla (ed.), *Mother Maria: Her Life and Letters* (Copyright DLT, 1979). Used by permission.

Sister Janet CSMV, *Mother Maribel of Wantage* (SPCK, 1973).

Thomas Merton, *Conjectures of a Guilty Bystander* (Burns & Oates, 1968, 1996). Used by permission of the publishers.

Edward Miall, *The British Churches in Relation to the British People* (1849).

J. G. Weber (ed. and trans.), *In Quest of the Absolute: The Life and Work of Jules Monchanin* (Kalamazoo: Cistercian Publications, and London: A. R. Mowbray & Co., Ltd, 1977).

L. Bradner and C. A. Lynch (eds and trans), *The Latin Epigrams of Thomas More* (Chicago, 1953).

William Morris in *Commonweal*, the magazine of the Socialist League, April 1885.

Edwin Muir, *An Autobiography* (Hogarth Press, 1987 edition). Used by permission.

Cecil Woodham-Smith, *Florence Nightingale* (Constable & Co., 1950).

Henri J. M. Nouwen, *With Burning Hearts: A Meditation on the Eucharistic Life* (Geoffrey Chapman, 1994).

John Oman, *Grace and Personality* (Cambridge University Press, 1917). Used by permission.

Raymond Lister, *The Paintings of Samuel Palmer* (Cambridge University Press, 1985).

A Religious of CSMV, *As in Adam: A Study in the Church* (A. R. Mowbray & Co., 1954).

Norman Penney (ed.), *Experiences in the Life of Mary Penington (written by herself)* (Philadelphia: The Biddle Press, and London: Headley Bros, 1911); copyright 1992, Friends Historical Society.

Karl Rahner, *Encounters with Silence*, trans. James M. Demske (Sands & Co., 1964).

Margaret Duggan (ed.), *Through the Year with Michael Ramsey: Devotional Readings for Every Day* (Triangle/SPCK, 1981).

R. M. Rilke, *Letters to a Young Poet*, trans. Reginald Snell (Sidgwick & Jackson, 1961).

John A. T. Robinson, *Honest to God* (SCM Press, 1963). Used by permission.

Oscar Romero, *The Church Is All of You: Thoughts of Archbishop Oscar Romero*, trans. James Brockman (Fount, 1985); copyright 1984, Chicago Province of the Society of Jesus.

Mark Rutherford, *More Pages from a Journal* (1910).

May Sarton, *Journal of a Solitude* (The Women's Press, 1985). Copyright 1973, May Sarton. Reprinted by permission of W. W. Norton & Co., Inc. and of the Women's Press.

Dorothy L. Sayers, 'Towards a Christian aesthetic' in *Unpopular Opinions* (Gollancz, 1946). By permission of David Higham Associates Ltd.

Vida Scudder, *On Journey* (E. P. Dutton & Co., Inc., 1937); copyright 1965, Fiduciary Trust Company. Used by permission of Penguin USA.

Logan Pearsall Smith (ed.) *A Religious Rebel: The Letters of H. W. Smith* (Nisbet, 1949). Used by permission of the publishers.

Adrienne von Speyr, *The Word: A Meditation on St John's Gospel*, trans. Alexander Dru (Collins, 1953).

Elizabeth Cady Stanton (ed.), *The Woman's Bible*, two vols. (New York: European Publishing Co., 1895–8).

Caroline Stephen, *Quaker Strongholds* (1890).

Pierre Teilhard de Chardin, *Hymne de l'univers*, copyright Editions du Seuil, 1961, trans. Simon Bartholomew (Collins, 1965). Used by permission.

John Casson, *Lewis and Sybil: A Memoir* (Collins, 1972).

R. S. Thomas, 'Kneeling', in *Not that He Brought Flowers* (J. M. Dent, 1968). Reproduced by permission.

Paul Tillich, *The Shaking of the Foundations* (SCM Press, 1949). Used by permission.

Philip Toynbee, *End of a Journey: An Autobiographical Journal 1979–81* (Bloomsbury, 1988). Used by permission.

Autobiography of George Tyrrell 1861–1884, published posthumously in 1912.

INDEX OF THEMES